THE
SKINNY MAN
LIVING IN THE DARK

THE
SKINNY MAN
LIVING IN THE DARK

DARRELL STROWDER

CITI OF
BOOKS

CITIOFBOOKS, INC.
3736 Eubank NE Suite A1
Albuquerque, NM 87111-3579
www.citiofbooks.com
Hotline: 1 (877) 389-2759
Fax: 1 (505) 930-7244

Ordering Information:
Quantity sales. Special discounts are available on quantity purchases by corporations, associations, and others. For details, contact the publisher at the address above.

Printed in the United States of America.

ISBN-13:	Softcover	979-8-89391-328-6
	eBook	979-8-89391-329-3

Library of Congress Control Number: 2024919765

TABLE OF CONTENTS

CHAPTER 01

I was born on January 5th, 1966, in Cleveland, Ohio. As a youngster, I was a badass little kid. I would always want attention. I had two brothers and two sisters and by me being the middle brother, I required a lot of attention. And when my little brother came into the world, he made it a little rough for me. I just wish he didn't ever come in because he was spoiled, a nice-looking kid and everybody loved him and I feel like I wasn't loved. So, I do things to show attention as being bad. My mother used to whip my ass a lot. I was just a badass. And I just felt like I was going to grow up to be nothing because my little brother took my place. But as I got older, I started developing the skills as I watched TV to say I wanted to be like somebody to make me have goals and be better. I tried that. It has been working for a long time for me being a youngster. I was a boy scout, a cub scout. I did basketball, boxing, karate. In baseball, I played on teams. I was pretty good. I was a left-hander.

But as I got older, becoming a teenager, that's when I saw myself going down the dark path. Because I was curious about a lot of things. My mother used to whip me so much that I stayed in trouble and told a lie. And I know I did it but I would lie so much that she said, you lie so much, you should be a lawyer. I would always get in trouble and get my ass whooped for no reason because I was just bad. But I had a skill. I was a hustler. My parents were poor but we survived through the storm. When I mean survive through the storm, we used to eat sometimes good meals, and sometimes we used to eat what we could. But at the end of the day, I would always go out and hustle, like, find little odd jobs as a little kid. It's just like, you need your bags carry home from the grocery stores and make me a couple dollars. Or I would hustle, pop bottles to take to the store to get candy. I was a great hustler.

So, then I realized that, I knew I had hustler skills. I went to school but I didn't finish school. I didn't finish high school. As far as I made it was to the ninth grade. I dropped out because I started being bad. I can tell you this. I was an athlete for playing sports. But that was not good enough for me. I wanted to get to women and had a nice car just like the players in the pimps. And I wanted to be cool. But then, once I started going that route, I started falling into this dark road of darkness and I never recovered. I was always getting into something. And I developed a skill that I had. My parents couldn't afford the things I wanted. So, I used to go to the stores and steal clothes. I got caught a bunch of times and I get my ass whooped. But I started getting good at it, so I never gave up. I kept getting it till I got it right because I thought I was untouchable.

So, when I started getting older, I was wearing the best designer clothes. Their money came back but I used to steal them. So, I knew that if I wore nice clothes, the women would like me because you got the guys to play basketball and you got the guys to play football and the women are always on their shoulders but I was like the skinny guy, so I feel like I was left out. And until I started wearing nice designer clothes, the girls used to ask me, where did you get that from? And they always thought that I was just on welfare and poor but they never knew. I was poor but I had nice clothes. So, I developed a skill, stealing clothes and I became a booster. And I was good at it until I got caught. At least I thought I was good until I got caught. I ended up getting locked up as a juvenile. And I saw all the bullies in jail in the detention home that I was scared of because I knew I wasn't the only bad person. After all, these were bad kids. But I got my skills tested by a big bully and I was scared of him but I was good with my hands. So, I whooped his ass and people gave me my respect.

CHAPTER 02

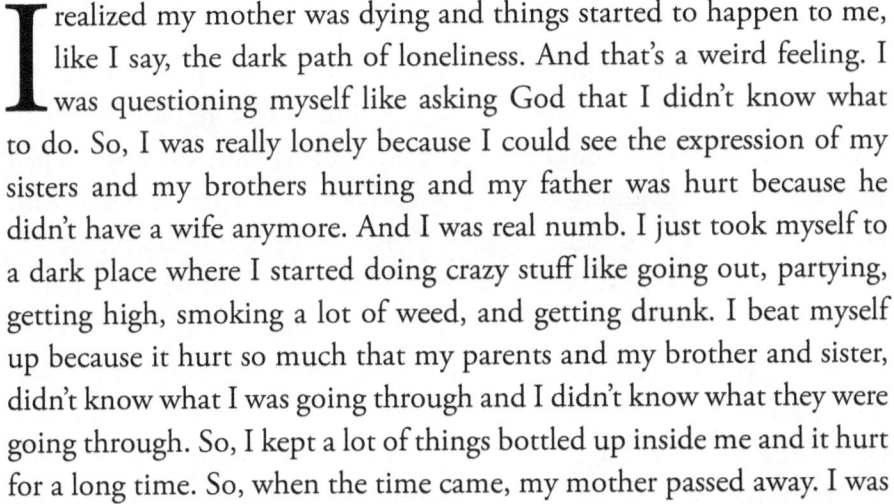

I realized my mother was dying and things started to happen to me, like I say, the dark path of loneliness. And that's a weird feeling. I was questioning myself like asking God that I didn't know what to do. So, I was really lonely because I could see the expression of my sisters and my brothers hurting and my father was hurt because he didn't have a wife anymore. And I was real numb. I just took myself to a dark place where I started doing crazy stuff like going out, partying, getting high, smoking a lot of weed, and getting drunk. I beat myself up because it hurt so much that my parents and my brother and sister, didn't know what I was going through and I didn't know what they were going through. So, I kept a lot of things bottled up inside me and it hurt for a long time. So, when the time came, my mother passed away. I was numb. I said a funeral. We all heard it, we cried. I didn't cry. I couldn't share a tear because I still was so hurt and numb. I didn't know what to do.

So, after the funeral, we had to repass at the house. All my aunts from New York and Alabama, and my grandmother, she kept us together. But when they left, we all fell apart again. Me and my brother were getting into it. I had another my oldest brother who was kind of disabled, he could understand what was going on. But me and my little brother, we began to fight each other because we had a lot of hurt. My two sisters seemed like they kind of were mature adults. Like, it didn't affect them much as it affected me and my little brother. Like my brother was 13 and I was 16. As the years went by, my father started to take a toll that he missed his wife because they bonded together and they did everything together and they had each other back. And that loneliness was taking a toll on my father. I don't know how he felt because I couldn't question him because we were all hurt but we got through it. My father sometimes would get drunk on the weekend and had his fits. And me and my brother would actually get into it again and fight and he used to break us up because we hated each other and we didn't know why.

And as we got older, I began to talk more to my sisters about death. They didn't give me too much to go on. I kind of figured it out as I got older, just knowing the spiritual, how we grew up in church. We went to church every Sunday. But I wasn't really into it because I was a hard-headed son. So, I would leave the church and go hang out with my friends. And sometimes I go hang out and stay out late and do bad stuff such as, I was doing crime. I would get in so much trouble with people, they used to call my parents. Well, my father was so tired of me. He sent me to New York in Brooklyn where my mother's sisters live for the summer and I stayed up there for the summer because I was so bad in Cleveland. And I lived in New York for the summer and it was different but my aunts never could control me. I was hanging out with my cousin and I was having fun at the time. I was hanging out with my cousin. When he'd get off work, we would go to the store and get a tray bag of weed that they used to sell and we would go sit on the stool and get high and drink this Montebello iced tea at the time.

And you know, the girls from New York used to tell me that I was country because I was from Cleveland, Ohio but they liked my swag because I was a skinny guy that loved to dress. I was wearing polo, YSL at that time and I was a young guy because I used to boost and I had a lot of clothes. So, at the time that I used to dress, I used to wear colorful clothes before the style became popular as this day. So, the girls used to like me. So, I had this one girl who liked me she was older, she was in the army and I was young and she had a daughter and she liked me but it was time for me to go back to Cleveland because time had gone past so fast and we used to sit out by the high school boys and girls and in the back and we used to just kiss each other and I really liked her because she had a nice body and she had that New York accent and I had that Cleveland accent so we made a perfect little match. But my aunt used to always tell me that girl is using you because you remind her of her baby's father. Y'all look resembling. I wasn't paying any attention to that. But I, down the stretch, it kind of, she was ripe. So, I finally went back to Cleveland to go back to school but I didn't go back to school. I used to run the streets. I used to tell my father I'm going to school and I'd go cut and hang out with the guys down the way in the projects.

And I used to hang with a lot of people down in the projects. We used to steal cars and hit licks, that was the thing to do because at that time it was all about the girls, like, when you have nice cars and stuff. So, our home with the guys was more on a different property level because they lived in a project and not live in a house. That's why we called it Down the Way. But once I got with this crew, I had that New York swag. And I was the leader and they loved me because I dressed. And I used to teach them a lot of things. And we used to go hit licks and they always used to bust and snatch. Like the cars that come from the freeway on their way going home. At rush hour, we will wait at a light, pick up a brick and bust their windows and snatch their purse, and run through the projects. And I never threw the brick. I was always telling them. I was, like, more the leader to signal out to which car to get and tell them who to hit because I was a strong guy.

I hung with the toughest guys in the projects. And I was the leader like I said before. They will always hit the licks, bust, snatch, and run through the projects. We find a location, break the purse down, and take all the stuff that's valuable out of it. Basically, we were looking for credit cards or money. We were looking for money. So, we would have the money and throw all the stuff away in the garbage can and we would go party and hang out. But I used to tell them, let me get my cut and I keep my cut and I save my money because I was more of the leader because they was a little bit slower than me and I had the ups on them. So, we will go to a place called Mr. Bee's. It was a game room and hang out and drink our beer and smoke a little weed and then we did party. We'll hang out and go home and do it again the next day.

CHAPTER 03

1983, a year later after my mom passed, we finally started picking our life back up. I thought it was hard grieving over our mother, losing our mother and we finally started taking a slow process of moving forward with our lives. It was still hard but one thing I can say is that I was still bitter about my mom leaving. I began by hanging out with some new friends that I grew up in the neighborhood with and the guys were called Junior Jackson. It was very popular. They would do talent shows and dancing and stuff like that. And they were pretty boys and they had all the girls. And I liked that because they were very talented and they had all the women. I felt like a little thug, but I had a little swag about myself because I used to hang with the guys down the way and I lead up to New York and learn some of their ways. And that's what made me different from everybody else in Cleveland. But we started hanging out, we would go to clubs like the Mad Hatter in the summertime and we would go to other clubs like the Coco Ballroom, City Lights, The Happy Apple, and Tweedy's. We had a little lot of things to do and we loved dancing. I loved dancing.

And the guys that I hung with, they loved dancing because they got the girls and so that kind of made me step my game up. And by me being skinny, it didn't matter because I was a sharp dresser. And I had good swag about myself so the girls started liking me too. But we will get drunk and go back down the way over to the girls' houses and kick it in and have sex and stuff like that. And before you know it, we go back home. And I had to sneak in because I stole my father's car to go out because nobody had a car. And I was the guy that took chances with my father. Even though he was very upset with me but I constantly would steal it because I was bad as hell. Only when I go out, and me and my father would get into it. We would argue and stuff. I respected my father but things that I wanted; I couldn't have. Because we grew up poor I had to earn it.

I was still a hustler, so I began to work the odd jobs to hustle and also again, the break-in houses to survive, the things that I wanted. And some of the guys that grew up around me, I would have them go into houses and break in them and take stuff like money, whatever valuable things and we would sell it. Until one day, somebody saw me breaking into a house across the street from me. And, they knew who I was because the other two guys that I had going to the house with me got caught and the person was in the house could have got killed but I got out and they got caught and they told on me. So, I was sitting at home watching Good Times, the show called Good Times and I heard a strange knock on the door. And my brother answered the door and it was the police. The Cleveland police were looking for me. So, I was scared and I knew what happened. They were looking for me. So, they took me to the fifth district in a holding cell and took me to Downtown to the DH.

CHAPTER 04

After I got out of DH, I was on probation. So, I had to start changing because I didn't like the ride I was taking. So, I began working at the Cleveland Stadium. I became a popcorn captain. That's where I got my street name from Popcorn. Everybody used to call me Popcorn. I worked under my brother's name, my oldest brother's name, John. Because I was too young to work down at the Cleveland Stadium but I had to hustle. So, I was very popular down at Cleveland Stadium because I became a captain and I did what I had to do. A lot of people respect me because I was the youngest guy down there but I was the oldest guy under somebody else's name. I work there selling popcorn at the Cleveland Stadium. I stopped working there. I began changing my life. I found a job at the Cleveland Clinic Hotel. I was a dishwasher. here. I worked there till 1988. I began hanging out with friends in the job, playing sports on our break and playing basketball. And we would hang out because they knew I was a cool little skinny guy who loved to be cool. I was a fly guy, so I was more the leader of the pack. So, I had a little crew there that I used to hang with. We used to go out on Cedar up to the job court where there's 107th Cedar Fair Hill for the girls to hang out. We used to take our little break to go up there and talk to the girls. And later on that week, we would hook up with some of them. We had a little bar that we used to go to on the 101st, Cedar that we used to hang out. And that's where the girls would be hanging out at the bar. So, we used to kick it and hang it.

Chapter 05

So, we used to hang out in my neighborhood. I had a little clubhouse where the job court women could come and hang out and kick back in and get high with us. We smoked weed, snorted cocaine, and listened to music. Some of them have sex but me myself, I wasn't into it like that. I was more on the serious side of making money. So, I used to sell a little bit of cocaine and sell a little bit of weed. Yeah, I was a good hustler. And one of the girls wanted to have sex with me but I wasn't liking her like that. So, I let my other dude have sex with her. Because the majority of the girls from job court come from a structure of messed-up homes. So, they go to job court the better they like. So, when they hang out, it's a different side of them on the freaky side. So, we gave them what they wanted. And they loved us Cleveland guys, especially me because I was the low-key skinny guy. They had a lot of things that they wanted. So, I began by helping them out giving them a couple of dollars. So, they can go back and tell their friends so they can bring more friends.

And then a lot of them will start coming around every weekend when we get off work during the weekend. And, one day I got into an argument with one of my friends. And he was kinda like way jealous of me because he couldn't do the things I did. He was bigger than me but I was the little guy that knew how to fight. I was good with my hands. And we got into a fistfight at my clubhouse and we kind of like we tore the clubhouse up and after that, we got back cool. He just wanted to prove a point and let people know that he was a tough guy and I wasn't nothing. I never said I was a tough guy. I was just a person that loved to hustle and be cool and have fun. But you put your hands on me, I'm gonna give you what you looking for. I was always the little guy who tried to get bullied because they felt like they could pick on me. Then the next time we hung out, we went to the bar that we used to go to on 101st. And the girls were up there that we used to hang out with and we used to just dance and have fun.

CHAPTER 06

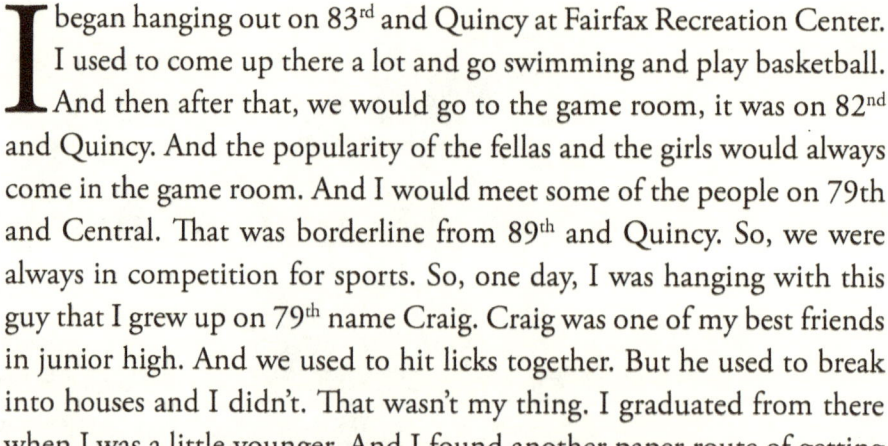

I began hanging out on 83rd and Quincy at Fairfax Recreation Center. I used to come up there a lot and go swimming and play basketball. And then after that, we would go to the game room, it was on 82nd and Quincy. And the popularity of the fellas and the girls would always come in the game room. And I would meet some of the people on 79th and Central. That was borderline from 89th and Quincy. So, we were always in competition for sports. So, one day, I was hanging with this guy that I grew up on 79th name Craig. Craig was one of my best friends in junior high. And we used to hit licks together. But he used to break into houses and I didn't. That wasn't my thing. I graduated from there when I was a little younger. And I found another paper route of getting money. So, me and him came tight and we hung out. And I know some of the people around 79th and Central didn't like me.

And I had friends from down the way, they were gangsters. They always liked me a lot and went to work for me. That's just the kind of person I was. So, one day, I came up to Fairfax to watch one of my friends play tennis. And my guy named Bo used to go with this chick named Bunny. I'm watching the girls play tennis. Then I see a group of guys from 79th and Central pull up on me. And they didn't like how I was moving because I was hanging with a person down the way but I'm cool with everybody. So, they circled me and told me my presence was welcome around Fairfax no more. And I grew up around these guys and went to school with some of these guys. So, they tell me that they don't like how I move and so they jump. Man, the guy sucker punched me first. I went to the ground. I didn't fall to the ground. My knees just buckled. And I began to cover up. And these guys got to punch me and beat me. And somewhere, somehow, that I got out from them jumping me and I ran home.

And I called my dude from down the way and told him what happened. He gets down the way guys, with these real gangsters and killers. I'd never carried a gun. So, they come down and meet me down there and they asked me where the guys at. So, I saw the guys but I didn't want any guns involved because all I had to do was point them out. They would have killed the guys that jumped me. I was kind of scared because I didn't believe in taking a life with guns. So, I played it off and said I don't see them. And then we left it like that and we skirted off. But I was hurt by it because these guys, I thought were cool and they were really, it showed real jealousy that I hang with different people. Like I owed them something. I didn't owe them anything to hang with anybody because I'm cool with everybody. I'm just a little skinny guy who's just cool with everybody. So, they didn't like that. So, they feel like they jumped me, just like really bullied me. So, I could have had them killed, but I didn't do it. So, I'm gonna leave it like that.

CHAPTER 07

1987, my son was one year old and time started getting a little different and it seemed like I couldn't stop chasing trouble. Trouble seems to find me as I got older. I mean, I would get in too much trouble for us, like starting to go to jail. When I go to jail, I get out and do the same thing. I didn't know no answer because I guess that the attention that I was looking for was the street and I got kind of street educated from learning a lesson by hanging out and getting involved in drugs and doing drugs. I was doing drugs like free-basing cocaine before I knew anything about crack. And then I graduated from free-basing to crack. And I started getting high with my sister. My sister introduced me to it.

And I used to wonder fuck some of her friends. Because they were nice and pretty and they had good jobs. And I wanted to try and see what it felt like. It felt good and I thought it was cool. So, I thought the drug that I was using started to take a toll on me. Now I'm seeing myself doing things that I thought I'd never do such as stealing for drugs to support my habit. And I got a kid who's one year old I really didn't pay attention to because this drug start getting me really hooked. And me and my kid's mother would get into it because she started finding symptoms of something weird about me and that's what about my addiction. And my addiction played a lot in a road of me not being successful. And I went into that dark space of loneliness because I didn't feel love. And drug was the only choice that I had that loved me.

CHAPTER 08

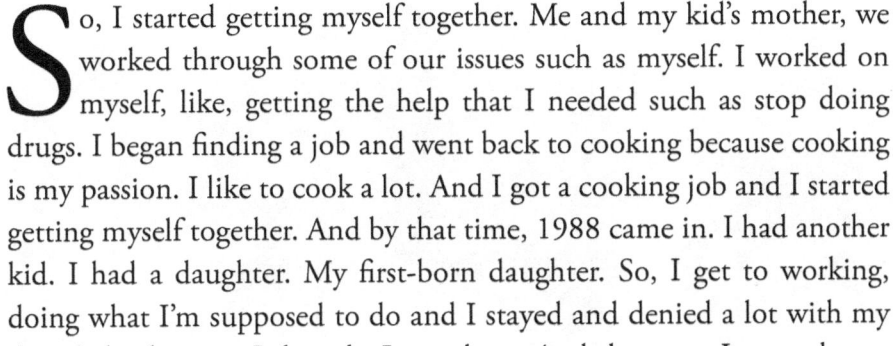

So, I started getting myself together. Me and my kid's mother, we worked through some of our issues such as myself. I worked on myself, like, getting the help that I needed such as stop doing drugs. I began finding a job and went back to cooking because cooking is my passion. I like to cook a lot. And I got a cooking job and I started getting myself together. And by that time, 1988 came in. I had another kid. I had a daughter. My first-born daughter. So, I get to working, doing what I'm supposed to do and I stayed and denied a lot with my drug habit because I thought I was done. And the more I try to better myself, the more that does. The demons will fight me to get back into that road again. So, I started using again. I kept my job but I started using.

So, I had to pay my bills but I was a closet smoker. You drink and can't handle your drinks and then you want to get high. So, at night time I would go out and hang out in club after 2:30. Me and a guy would go buy some dope and people never thought that I smoked crack, cocaine because of my appearance. I was skinny and I dressed and I was real groomed. I kept myself together. And I knew I was doing wrong. And then I was jeopardizing my family. I didn't care. It got worse. So, I started doing things again like, hitting licks to feed my family. Some of the money I would take when I hit licks, I'd take care of home and then I'd rush the money, I'd go blow. I had it kind of under control but

I really didn't because I was fooling myself that I thought I had this drug under control. Down the stretch it really whooped be.

CHAPTER 09

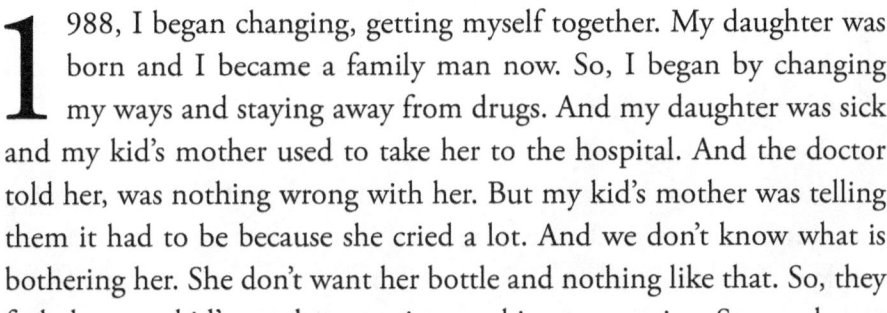

988, I began changing, getting myself together. My daughter was born and I became a family man now. So, I began by changing my ways and staying away from drugs. And my daughter was sick and my kid's mother used to take her to the hospital. And the doctor told her, was nothing wrong with her. But my kid's mother was telling them it had to be because she cried a lot. And we don't know what is bothering her. She don't want her bottle and nothing like that. So, they feel that my kid's mother was just making up stories. So, we began questioning that. I was questioning that why every time she t hollering or something.

And I'm at work and she was telling, she at the hospital and I would get upset. I had a cute little daughter too, Talisha. And I used to get upset with my kids' mother. We'd get in arguments and they'd get heated. And make a long story short, my daughter was diagnosed with cerebral palsy. It messed me up. Because I didn't understand what Cerebral Palsy was and what not. And so, they had to keep her for do more testing on her and somehow, they end up taking my daughter from my kids' mother. And we started getting into it because I was arguing with her about why just kept going to the hospital or whatever. And she was diagnosed with cerebral palsy, like I said, again and she is in this place where they can take care of her. And me and my kid's mother would go see her every day.

CHAPTER 10

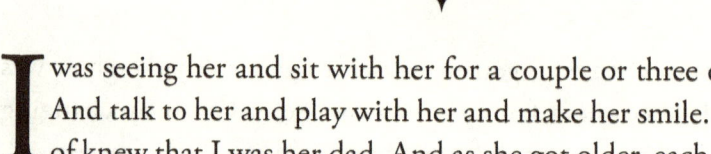

I was seeing her and sit with her for a couple or three or four hours. And talk to her and play with her and make her smile. And she kind of knew that I was her dad. And as she got older, each day she knew that I was coming. And the nurses know that when I come to visit her, her moods changed because I was motivating her and it was motivating me more. So that made me slowdown from the street life because I thought that karma came back and bit me in the ass. That's the way I look at it. I couldn't question God. I thought about all the things that I did. I was neglecting my kids, my two kids at the time, probably running in the street. So, I had to get myself together because my kids need me and my kid's mother need me. And I knew they'd do the right thing. But down the stretch things start to get worsen. My daughter started having seizures and stuff and one day I came and visited her, they wouldn't let me see her and I'm like, what's going on? They couldn't tell me. And I get upset, I start flipping out and my kid's mother was crying and I tried to console her but I was more hurt.

So, they had to take her to another place where they can treat her better. So, they took her to another place where she can get treated. I would still come visit her every day when she, the same regular, she was back together but they had these tubes in her to feed her and they always had her wired up that she can really just see me and smile but I didn't want to see my daughter with all these little wires and tubes on her and I didn't know what cerebral palsy was. To me, they just came up with a name because it's popular now. I didn't know what the term was, what it was before. But I was starting to feel trapped and hurt again because my daughter could never come home because we didn't have the facility and equipment to take care of our daughter. So, every day we'd visit her. And I visit her more because I was glued onto my daughter because of her condition. It changed me a lot, it really did.

Chapter 11

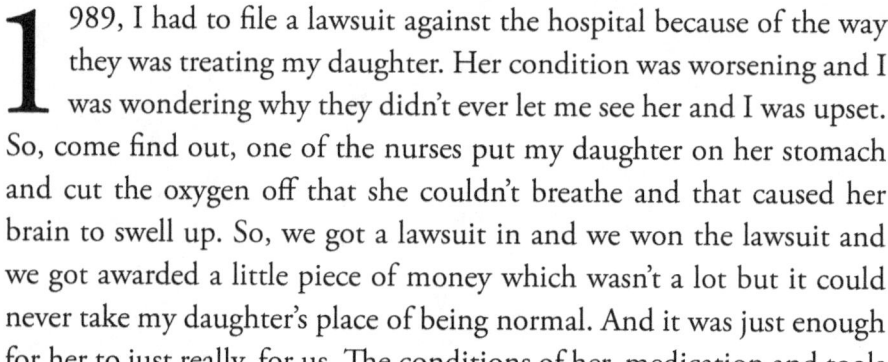

1989, I had to file a lawsuit against the hospital because of the way they was treating my daughter. Her condition was worsening and I was wondering why they didn't ever let me see her and I was upset. So, come find out, one of the nurses put my daughter on her stomach and cut the oxygen off that she couldn't breathe and that caused her brain to swell up. So, we got a lawsuit in and we won the lawsuit and we got awarded a little piece of money which wasn't a lot but it could never take my daughter's place of being normal. And it was just enough for her to just really, for us. The conditions of her, medication and tools all hooked up to her, it kind of, really freaked me out and that she had to be like this the rest of her life.

So, I began to feel depressed. And by me being on drugs, I relapsed. I had gotten myself together but it was hurting so much that I would just get high to take the pain away, at one point in time just to like, end my life because I didn't want my daughter to suffer like that but I knew that my family needed me. So, I just went on a bench for a little bit of a period of time and I came back to reality to get myself together but I still was hurt. I don't know why certain things happened, but I can't question that. I just had to take the bitter with the sweet. So, I began by taking it one day at a time.

CHAPTER 12

1 990, another year went past. I received a phone call from my sister telling me that my grandmother passed. I wouldn't really expect to hear that but we had to regroup and get ready to go back down south to Alabama to bury our grandmother and visit our cousins and rest of the family. It was sad but we got through it. We pulled through. And we went our separate ways after the funeral. We go back home. I go back home to Cleveland, Ohio. My family go back to New York, my aunts. And when I came back to Cleveland, Ohio, I know my kid's mother was pregnant. She was six months. I got another daughter that's on the way, my second daughter. I began still doing my one-two, such as working and being a good guy. But sometimes, me and my kid's mother, we live together, we would have a little conflict but one day it got into an argument that it got to that she had called the police on me. It wasn't no physical argument; it was a verbal argument.

Police came and they calmed the situation down but they had to run a check on me and find out that I had a warrant. So, they had to take me into custody. So, now that I know I had a warrant for RSP; receiving stolen property, I end up doing a little time. I do a year in penitentiary, pick away correctional institution. By that time, my daughter was born when I was incarcerated. I begin doing in time and when I was locked up, I became an indigent such as I didn't have no income coming in from the outside world so I had to hustle. And inside I had to make ends meet. The best way I knew how so by me just knowing when my

21

back against the wall, I became a barber. I didn't know too much about cutting hair but I was good with my hands and in regulation haircuts wasn't too hard to do. It was just a part that doing other people's hair they want a ball-face style haircuts. So, I tried it and I messed a couple people up but I got better down the stretch. And almost got my ass kicked by certain people cutting their hair. And I messed their hairs up but I got better.

So, I started making a little money like getting packs of cigarettes, goodies, stuff like that. So, I didn't really need nothing from my family from the outside world because I started making a name for myself as a hustler. So, I wish I felt good about myself but I'd rather just see my family send me money but I didn't have too many people out there in my corner. A lot of people wanted to see me down and out anyway. So, I learned from my mistakes behind that. So, I just did my time to try to come home but I had got into a fight with one guy from Cleveland and he tried to chump me out because he thought that he was cocky and strong, that he can talk to me. So, we got into a heated argument because one of my guys left to go back to court to Cleveland and he asked me to collect his debts that people owed him a two for one. So, I collect them. So, to come find out the guy that he gave a pack of cigarettes to, he wanted them and he told him, collected from me. So, I gave him a pack of cigarettes but he wanted to collect the two for ones. He wanted more like he was extorting me. I gave him what my guy gave him. So, we got into it, he sucker punched me and stabbed me in my eye with his fingernail.

And when I saw blood, I tore his ass up. I hit him with a three-piece, one body shot and two jabs. And they broke it up because the correction also was coming. So, we split up and we go into the bathroom to really finish it. But we just, like say, you got the best of me and I got the best of you. We're going to leave it like that. So, I had to go to a hospital for my eye and they asked me what happened because I can go to the hole and get a hole shot. But I didn't go. So, I maneuvered and said I got poked in the eye accidentally playing baseball. So, they take me to an outside hospital called OSU Hospital in Columbus. So, it was like a graze that his fingernail hit my eyeball and it caused my vision to get blurry. So, I had to wear a patch over my eye till it get better. So, I got back and I really was heated. I wanted to get the guy but by that time, the word spreaded that I got out on him. It's like that skinny dude got out on you which I wasn't bragging about it. I just was protecting myself and trying to hold down a fork because when you get locked up, if you get your ass whooped, you're gonna be labeled.

So, I did what I had to do. So, we squashed that and I went on and doing my time and I had to get myself together to go home. I had a daughter, another daughter to take care of. So, when I got home, I was glad to see my youngest daughter, my second youngest daughter rather. And I felt good about that. So, I began doing the right thing for a minute, but me and my kids' mother get back together. We try to raise our kids together but things weren't working out because the man is supposed to be the provider and the wife is supposed to take care of the kids. So, I'm working a regular job. It wasn't enough money to come in. So, I started doing side hustle. I got back into my old ways. Money was coming in pretty good. And, I was selling weed and cocaine. I catch a case and again, I get caught up. And by that time, I'm just fighting my case. And that was that for right now.

CHAPTER 13

1991 and 1992, I'm fighting my case. Now I'm on the run. And, me and my kids mother broke up but I end up getting her pregnant again. I end up having a third daughter, my youngest daughter. And I'm on the run. So, I lived with this young lady that I was kicking it with. Me and her was just like a, she was my sap, put it like that. And she ended up being my woman because I really liked her and she had a lot of potentials. So, I ended up moving in with her. She was nice looking, everything. And I moved in with her out by the airport and it's called the Rocky River Apartments by the airport. So, now me and her kicking it and everything but I know I got a warrant because I'm on the run. I skipped by. So, they called my people. The body hunters called my people where I was living at and whatever and then nobody know where I was staying at. So, I was staying with my girlfriend and we had a good bond but I knew I had to fight this case and on the run. So, my brother got me out on bond but I guess he forfeit the bond. They had to pay the money and what not.

So, my brother ended up telling on me where I was located. So, I'm laying up in the bed and I see some cars pull up. I hear some noise. So, I look out the window and I'm upstairs. And they jumped out the car and I knew they was for me. So, they surround the house and knock on the door. So, I opened the top window like I was about to jump out. By this time my girlfriend answered the door and let them in. So, I barricade myself in a closet and put clothes on me or the laundry clothes on me so they wouldn't find me. And I make them think that I jumped out the window. So, one guy looked in the closet, I guess he saw my body parts moving. So, he, like, had a Chrome 357 shining at me and telling me to come out now. And I had on my shorts and my girl house shoes. And they pulled me up out of there and it was really embarrassing. They took me to jail with my girl house shoes on and shorts on. And I asked them, can I put my clothes on or whatever for you to take me down. Don't let me go down like this. They didn't. By me being a little skinny dude, they was trying to rough me up and press my girl, like, you should have thought about that shit when you was; only you know what you did. And I'm like, man, y'all got me, let me put my clothes on, let me put some clothes on before I go to jail. Y'all gonna take me like this.

So, they bum rush me, put me in the car, took me to jail. And come find out, one of the bounty hunters tried to knock my girlfriend off. He come back to the house, my girlfriend come visit me and tell me that bounty hunter tried to talk to her and he wanted to take her out and I said, man, you can't win for trying, boy. So, I said, well, if you feel like that's the right move and you want to leave me, I ain't nothing I can do. I'll be hurt but I get over it but I just need somebody to be in my corner while I do this time. So, I didn't know I was gonna do time. So, I get probation somehow and I get out. And by that time, me and my kids' mother, we try to communicate a little bit because now my other daughter is about to be born. So, she was born and we really went seeing eye to eye with each other so we end up breaking up and by that time, I think I relapsed. I started back getting high because things wouldn't go my way.

So, I, you know, when things don't go your way, results to turn to drugs. So, I ended up doing drugs again and because I knew I was about to go to penitentiary again. And I was kind of lost out there. I was in love with two women, my kid's mother and this other lady that I was with. And the girl I was with, she really did me, but she had a lot of issues going with herself financially. And I couldn't, I was trying to provide for both her and my baby mama but I couldn't. I was managing it because

I had good character by myself, but you know, I was hurting so much that I, you know, like I just said, getting high and I knew I was on the run. So, eventually I didn't give a fuck and I end up getting locked up for a dirty urine. And I ended up doing time again. So, I get locked up, I get it. I'm back doing my regular, like being in jail, being a barber, making my little hustle because I know ain't nobody gonna look out for me. And I'm in the county jail hustling till I get to my parent institution and I get a letter. When I get to my receiving institution, it's Lorraine. I get a letter from my girlfriend. She sent me a dear John letter that she don't wanna be bothered with me no more. So, I'm kinda hurt because I know my kid's mother didn't found somebody or whatever. So, I'm, you know, I'm in a cell going through it about her.

So, one day, the white shirt come and visit me to my cell. The white shirt is like the captain. And I thought I did something wrong in the end, you know, because we were locked down for seven days and only time you come out your cells to eat. So, he come and asked me, Mr. Strowder, we need to talk to you. And I was like okay, what about? So, they took me down to this little room. And I'm thinking all the stuff that I did. I said, I done got another case. I don't know whatever I did. And he tell me, December 08, 1992, my sister get killed. He told me that my sister got into an accident and she died. And I'm like, what you mean she died? So, they let me call home and I talked to my aunt and my other sister and they told me what happened. So, by that time I'm blown away. They told me what happened. They are like, yeah, she passed away. And I'm like, really what happened? They didn't really want to tell me, but you know, you find out more stuff in the penitentiary than you find out more in the streets. So, some way, somehow, I found out what happened to my sister. My sister get killed.

Her and this lady was fighting and she stabbed my sister to death about 17 times because she couldn't beat my sister. So, she stabbed her. And it was over drugs and she died on the line in front of my father, on the line and man, you know, when I found out how it happened, I was confused. So, now I done lost my girlfriend and I lost my sister and

26

nothing I can do. I'm stuck from a hard rock in a hard place. And I don't know what to do. So, I kept myself together. I didn't clock out or nothing like that or flip out. I just held it in and I went to the funeral. Not the funeral, I went to visit. They let me go visit my sister, see her body and everything. And I got back to my institution and by that time I'd get shipped out to Marion Correctional. So, now I'm doing my turn. You know, they give me two years. I do two years. And in the meantime, I had to just better myself now because all these things that happened to me and these are wake-up calls that I'm just thinking like God is trying to tell you something to wake up, get your life together.

So, I'm doing my time, getting myself together, gaining a little weight, feeling good. You know, I mean, I am going to school and just trying to upgrade myself and be a better person this time. And down the stretch, I get another visit from a white shirt in Marion. This in 1994 doing to my two years that I did. So, they told me, my daughter my oldest daughter passed away. And I'm like, wow, you serious? So, now I'm really lost. Nobody can console me. I can't turn to nobody but God. And I can't question God. But I knew my daughter had health issues, so she passed away. And at a young age, so I'm devastated. I don't know which way to go. So, I go visit her body and they let me go visit her. So now that the lawsuit, it came through and we won the case. So, they had an administrator to divide the money between my kids' mother and me.

So, we would get a cheque once a month. So, I got something to come home to, now. So, it's just like this, I ain't gotta work that hard or whatever. So, I had about like about 50,000 will not get out. I got out in 1995. So, I got a little money from my daughter, deceased. And so, I didn't have to really go too hard in the paint to work and get on my feet. So, by that time I got on my feet a little bit, brought me a car, got me a little wardrobe, a little jewelry and what not. And I was toned up and then, you know, I go to New York, go buy some clothes, you know, start hustling it. No more just selling drugs. Now I'm back into selling clothes again, you know, because I used to be a booster. So now I'm selling clothes. I'm selling all the fashion from Tommy Hilfiger,

Nautica, Polo, you name it. I got it. So, now I'm this businessman I supposed to be and I end up doing that.

CHAPTER 14

Things started to go good for me now since I started selling clothes. I'm grossing a thousand dollars a week and I'm very happy about it. I'm going back and forth to Cleveland and New York and I'm having fun along the way. I take the Greyhound every trip and I got back to Cleveland and I met a young lady in the Tower City, wreckage shop, Celek Wreck. She was very attractive and I really thought I couldn't talk to her but when I brought my CD's, I brought the Earth, Wind, Fire and the Isley Brothers, we had a nice little conversation. Somehow that I got her phone number, she gave me her number. And I took a while to call her but I finally did because my business was going good. And I took her out. We had fun and things started to take courses of like we were hooking up every day and her conversation was real strong.

Her intellect was so amazing that it made me very attractive to her. So, I began by taking her to dinner and she had two kids, a son and a daughter. They was young at the time but her ex-boyfriend was a correction officer. And he used to be harassing her because she broke up with him. And I'm the new guy in her life. And you know, he was giving her a little hard time so one day he called on the phone, cussing her out. And I got the phone and told him like, look my man, she got somebody else. Why don't you just fall back and accept it that she moved on? So, that's all he needed to hear and he respected. We didn't get into no confrontation about it, no arguments or nothing. He respected and he never called no more. So, we started hitting it off and she liked it at about me because I was a stand-up guy.

CHAPTER 15

I really liked her and we began seeing more and more of each other. And you know, she's going to school to get her PhD in science and she worked two jobs at the record store in the BP building. And I still had a lot going on as far as my hustling, going back and forth to selling clothes to New York to Cleveland. I just feel like that at that time, I still had other women was digging me and I put them to the side. I was into her because I'm a one woman's man. My old girlfriend tried to get back in my life, jump back in the car with me but I wasn't having that. Because she heard that I'm doing good and she wanted to get back in the car with me. So, that wasn't going to happen. So, I end up going through another trial and tribulation. I was with my nephew one day in East Cleveland. I was going to the store. I wanted to walk. And it was late at night. And I seen a Delta 88 prime black car and they rolled past first and then they circled around again and as I came back from the store they jumped out of the car with the bandanas on around their face and they robbed me. They tried to rob me, put it like that. I had my money in my shoes. I had on some Jordans and I had on a nice little short outfit.

The guys got out and asked me where is that. He took my chain off my neck. I had a little rope chain and what not and they're like where the money at? I'm like I don't know what you're talking about man. We just going to the store and my nephew that lived in East Cleveland he took off running. So, that made the four guys pissed with me. The guy smacked me in the face with a pistol, hit me on the bridge of my eye, corner of my eye, blood gushing out. And I'm like, man, I ain't got no money. I had money but I wasn't giving it up. So, he clicked it, pulled the gun out and he said, I'm going to ask you one more time. And he's like, told me to take off everything. And I'm just holding my side of my eye. And I'm like, man. Come on now, man, it's really worth it. And he like saved me with that Dr. Martin Luther King speech. So, he hit me again on the bridge of my nose. So, I kinda lost it. I saw blood everywhere now. So, and I'm like, man, I ain't got it. You hit me with that pistol one more time, man. I'm telling you because it hurt so bad. I just clocked out and then he pulled the trigger and the pistol jammed. The gun jammed. He was about to take my life and then off-duty police rode past and seen the situation and he jumped out of the car and they skirted off. And I had to go to the hospital, get stitches. And I was really upset because I had to tell my new girlfriend what happened and my family, what happened. And, you know, it was real bad.

CHAPTER 16

Me and my new girlfriend was starting to get real serious with each other. Her feelings were getting strong. The minds were getting strong too. But in back of my head, I had doubts about getting serious with a woman because my ex-girlfriend left me for dead when I was incarcerated. So, I was real skeptical about my feelings. But my feelings developed anyway with her because she was so attractive and she won me over and I won her over. And during the mistletoe of the storm, she nursed me back to health. So that was much love for her. So, I began by taking her to school at Tracey on 30th Community College and dropped her off and she wanted me to pick her back up later on. It was snowing that day; it was like a real blizzard. And I'm doing my errands at that time, selling clothes and what not. I get a call from my ex-girlfriend so she wanted to meet up with me and talk. So, I meet up with her because I still had feelings for her but my feelings weren't that strong with her no more because she left me for dead when I was incarcerated and I'll never forget that. So, I was on some revenge type stuff to get back at her.

So, I met with her and we talked and what not and you know she was looking good and stuff and telling me how she feels and how she really was like vulnerable at that time but it was no excuse. I really needed her. So, I told her I moved on and got me somebody else and she understood. But she said she would never give up on me and try to put the relationship back together. So, I just felt like, I was trying to live the best of having two women. And so, I later on that day, I hanging out with her and time went back so fast that I forgot to pick her up. Because I, kind of, was out getting high far as drinking and I smoked a wet joint. And that's what took me out of the game that way. So, I dropped her off and I fell asleep in my car. And I woke up, it was dark. She blowing my pager up and I realized like why I forgot about to pick her up. And I made an excuse and said something happened. And I was with another woman because I wasn't always faithful with that relationship. Because I was just seeing another woman to see if me and her still had that bond but we didn't. I just wanted to get over that bond with her because I was just still confused.

Chapter 17

Me and my new girlfriend was starting to get real serious with each other. Her feelings were getting strong. The minds were getting strong too. But in back of my head, I had doubts about getting serious with a woman because my ex-girlfriend left me for dead when I was incarcerated. So, I was real skeptical about my feelings. But my feelings developed anyway with her because she was so attractive and she won me over and I won her over. And during the mistletoe of the storm, she nursed me back to health. So that was much love for her. So, I began by taking her to school at Tracey on 30th Community College and dropped her off and she wanted me to pick her back up later on. It was snowing that day; it was like a real blizzard. And I'm doing my errands at that time, selling clothes and what not. I get a call from my ex-girlfriend so she wanted to meet up with me and talk. So, I meet up with her because I still had feelings for her but my feelings weren't that strong with her no more because she left me for dead when I was incarcerated and I'll never forget that. So, I was on some revenge type stuff to get back at her.

So, I met with her and we talked and what not and you know she was looking good and stuff and telling me how she feels and how she really was like vulnerable at that time but it was no excuse. I really needed her. So, I told her I moved on and got me somebody else and she understood. But she said she would never give up on me and try to put the relationship back together. So, I just felt like, I was trying to live the best of having two women. And so, I later on that day, I hanging out with her and time went back so fast that I forgot to pick her up. Because I, kind of, was out getting high far as drinking and I smoked a wet joint. And that's what took me out of the game that way. So, I dropped her off and I fell asleep in my car. And I woke up, it was dark. She blowing my pager up and I realized like why I forgot about to pick her up. And I made an excuse and said something happened. And I was with another woman because I wasn't always faithful with that relationship. Because I was just seeing another woman to see if me and her still had that bond but we didn't. I just wanted to get over that bond with her because I was just still confused.

Chapter 18

My hustle started going good for me, so good for me that I started to go out and to the clubs and meet other women, take them back to the hotel, have sex with them and just leave them from that day. But to one day, my ex-girlfriend called me and we get together. And she gave me an ultimatum about our relationship, which we didn't have one. But I thought about it and we started seeing each other again. So, let me talk about the ultimatum. She told me that she will die for me. And I ask what you mean, you will die for me? She said she'd take a bullet for me. So, I was like, wow. You are saying all this now and when I needed you wasn't there for me. I was hurt. She was serious with what she said. So, we end up seeing each other more and more. We got back together. And, I don't know that I've made a bad mistake. But things she said, she meant what she said. She was down for me.

I get into an altercation with a guy about some clothes. And she was right there with me and she ended up checking the guy for me. And the guy probably thought I was a little bitch or something because he told me that you got your woman standing up for you. And I'm like saying you know what, I can handle you but my girl just jumped in it and told the dude like, we ain't want that. You need to go head on with that bullshit. So, make a long story short, the guy felt offended. So, he really wanted to fight me because my girl got involved in the conversation. And I handled it. We just argued and did no blows get thrown. We just left it like that and I went on about my business because he gonna tell me my stuff was knockoff. And I'm like, I don't sell knockoff stuff. I get mine from a distributor, where you don't know where I get my stuff from. You may say I go to New York but I had nice people that hook me up with the real stuff. And I do not knock off from the real. So, that's how that went about.

So, now a couple months go by, we're going into 1996. I like still going back and forth to New York. So, to clear to New York, I have a place. So, I moved at a hotel called a charter house. So, I've been there for almost a good while. I used to have my kids come out there and swim. My son, he loved to swim a lot. And my daughters, they looked tiny but they were swimming too. But we didn't have too much of the shallow water. So, it was like four feet. They learned how to swim because their brother taught them how to swim a little bit. Me and my girlfriend, we would be on a patio balcony watching them from a distance. We would just live our best life at that time. I used to just feed my kids a lot of fast food, whatever they wanted because I didn't have accessories of stove and kitchen. They had some rooms with them but I didn't. I wanted the pool side where they had the outside patios because it was nice and it was convenient for me. And I had people come over and think I was just doing my thing which I was and what not. And I just took one day at a time with my ex-girlfriend. We started to fall in love again and it got real serious. And one day, I was riding by myself, taking a customer some clothes and I ran into my girlfriend that I broke up with. She was still looking decent and everything happy. But I stopped and said hi to her. And, she had met somebody else and I was happy for her. And we went on our ways.

CHAPTER 19

In 1996, me and my girlfriend living in a charter house out Euclid, Ohio. She get a job as housekeeping. And I'm just doing my regular hustle. And one day, I got up in the morning and I heard one of the housekeeping ladies. Grandkids was out there swimming. And she was hollering and my girlfriend told me, Darrell, come, come quick. I get up and looked out the balcony. And I see kids standing around the pool. And I jumped off my balcony and I see a little kid at the bottom of the water at the drain. And I dived in and pulled the kid out. And put him on the surface and pumped his chest. And I told his grandmother to get him mouth to mouth for him to come out alive. I saved a little guy's life. I was so hurt that I thought about my kids. And she thanked me. And I didn't need no thanking because if my kids would have been in that situation, I would expect somebody to do the same for me. So, there was God on my side. It just fortunately happened that I was at the right place at the right time to help this little kid save his life. So, now we move on to the next level of the day, getting up, getting something to eat and hit the streets and go out and hustle. And my girl, she in there working because I had to tell her, get her game up and get some income coming in so we can go to the next level. Everything's working out pretty fine for us. And I just take my time.

CHAPTER 20

My hustle started going good for me, so good for me that I started to go out and to the clubs and meet other women, take them back to the hotel, have sex with them and just leave them from that day. But to one day, my ex-girlfriend called me and we got together. And she gave me an ultimatum about our relationship, which we didn't have one. But I thought about it and we started seeing each other again. So, let me talk about the ultimatum. She told me that she will die for me. And I ask what you mean, you will die for me? She said she'd take a bullet for me. So, I was like, wow. You are saying all this now and when I needed you wasn't there for me. I was hurt. She was serious with what she said. So, we end up seeing each other more and more. We got back together. And, I don't know that I've made a bad mistake. But things she said, she meant what she said. She was down for me.

I get into an altercation with a guy about some clothes. And she was right there with me and she ended up checking the guy for me. And the guy probably thought I was a little bitch or something because he told me that you got your woman standing up for you. And I'm like saying you know what, I can handle you but my girl just jumped in it and told the dude like, we ain't want that. You need to go head on with that bullshit. So, make a long story short, the guy felt offended. So, he really wanted to fight me because my girl got involved in the conversation. And I handled it. We just argued and did no blows get thrown. We just left it like that and I went on about my business because he gonna tell me my stuff was knockoff. And I'm like, I don't sell knockoff stuff. I get mine from a distributor, where you don't know where I get my stuff from. You may say I go to New York but I had nice people that hook me up with the real stuff. And I do not knock off from the real. So, that's how that went about.

So, now a couple months go by, we're going into 1996. I like still going back and forth to New York. So, to clear to New York, I have a place. So, I moved at a hotel called a charter house. So, I've been there for almost a good while. I used to have my kids come out there and swim. My son, he loved to swim a lot. And my daughters, they looked tiny but they were swimming too. But we didn't have too much of the shallow water. So, it was like four feet. They learned how to swim because their brother taught them how to swim a little bit. Me and my girlfriend, we would be on a patio balcony watching them from a distance. We would just live our best life at that time. I used to just feed my kids a lot of fast food, whatever they wanted because I didn't have accessories of stove and kitchen. They had some rooms with them but I didn't. I wanted the pool side where they had the outside patios because it was nice and it was convenient for me. And I had people come over and think I was just doing my thing which I was and what not. And I just took one day at a time with my ex-girlfriend. We started to fall in love again and it got real serious. And one day, I was riding by myself, taking a customer some clothes and I ran into my girlfriend that I broke up with. She was still looking decent and everything happy. But I stopped and said hi to her. And, she had met somebody else and I was happy for her. And we went on our ways.

CHAPTER 21

In 1996, me and my girlfriend living in a charter house out Euclid, Ohio. She get a job as housekeeping. And I'm just doing my regular hustle. And one day, I got up in the morning and I heard one of the housekeeping ladies. Grandkids was out there swimming. And she was hollering and my girlfriend told me, Darrell, come, come quick. I get up and looked out the balcony. And I see kids standing around the pool. And I jumped off my balcony and I see a little kid at the bottom of the water at the drain. And I dived in and pulled the kid out. And put him on the surface and pumped his chest. And I told his grandmother to get him mouth to mouth for him to come out alive. I saved a little guy's life. I was so hurt that I thought about my kids. And she thanked me. And I didn't need no thanking because if my kids would have been in that situation, I would expect somebody to do the same for me. So, there was God on my side. It just fortunately happened that I was at the right place at the right time to help this little kid save his life. So, now we move on to the next level of the day, getting up, getting something to eat and hit the streets and go out and hustle. And my girl, she in there working because I had to tell her, get her game up and get some income coming in so we can go to the next level. Everything's working out pretty fine for us. And I just take my time.

CHAPTER 22

Everything going great. Me and my girl working her job in the housekeeping and we getting a discount for staying in a hotel and the money wasn't no problem about me paying. But we living in a hotel, we didn't got cool with the people that run it because it was some Lebanese people that own the hotel. So, they let us pay, like, monthly and my girl work in housekeeping. So, we had a good leverage. My kids come out every day to swim. My son, he stays in the water all day, every day. My daughter, they like helping my girlfriend in housekeeping, doing some of the rooms, doing the lady chores and it's helping them learn the value and responsibility doing chores. And myself, I'm just kicked back doing my hustle. I started working a job too. I got back into cooking again to keep an extra income. Because the clothes was good but I still needed an extra income. Because I like to do things and spend money, just as well, my kids, they growing up and things that they like, I make sure they had the best of things but I make them understand the value of material stuff such as clothes is a privilege.

And one day, I get a call from my father. My father was like my best friend. He was a good guy. He was very intelligent, a lot of wisdom, a lot of knowledge that old school soul. So, we talking and what not. And he had to go to the veteran hospital. And he was telling me things about his health. And I was just telling him that you're going to be okay. Just stay strong, keep doing what you're doing whatever, going to dialysis and taking the treatments or whatever he was supposed to do, he was doing it. My father had it, a good life. I went around February, 1997. No, 96. Take that back, 96. I give him a birthday party. I heard, my father was turning 70. And I hired some strippers. I know my father wasn't into that but he was an active guy. So, I was just showing him a good time. I got some strippers and made the strippers give him a lap dance and his friends; they enjoyed it. They're old schools and they ain't never really been around in situations like that. So, I made sure all of them had a lap dance. I was just watching them and smiling and like, wow, these guys is having a good time, real OGs.

Chapter 23

The best was yet to come. I fighted my family over, my brother, my nephews. We had a swimming contest, who can dive the best. Because they always thought they could swim better than me and dive better than me. I'm the oldest. And so, we got it on. So, we all swam and dived. Because we grew up at Fairfax Recreation Center 83rd and Central, Cleveland, Ohio, we all used to go to this recreation center and go swimming. And my thing was, they didn't know I had a summer job as a lifeguard. And I knew how to swim a little better because I feel like, by me being skinny, that my dives was like a bird with wings. And I looked so good when I dived. I could have been in a lift. But I was impressed about my brother and my nephew dives too also. They really showed up. And we had a good time. My kids watching and learning something. And later on we ate pizza and beer, laughed, taught, listened to music. And my girlfriend, she was at work. She was very jealous hearted because she couldn't participate but you can't be at everything. So now, later on, we go hang out. I take the kids somewhere to get babies to their mother's house so she can watch them while me and the fellas go hang out. We go to BW3s and drink some beers and eat wings also, just to watch sports.

CHAPTER 24

So, later on that day, me and my brother, we get ready to go out. We go to the Park Avenue in East Cleveland. We go there and it was a little place at that time. I just wanted to go dancing. Me and him both wanted to do our little thing, go out and have some fun. And I had a good time, no fights, no nothing, it jumped off, it was just a cool day. Most of the times, fights jump off in East Cleveland. But didn't happen, transpired. So, we had a little fun and we went our separate ways. So, I go home, kick back with my girl, wait for the next day and go to work. I'm working at Bob Big Boys Out, Euclid, Babbit Road. Later that day, a couple of the OGs came in and they ordered some food. They gave a confirmation back of the house, which is me. They liked the food. They gave me a $100 tip which I appreciated. It makes me feel that I can touch people's stomachs and they taste good. So, I felt good out doing my thing. I got home, get changed, tell my girl, let's go out and celebrate a little bit. So, we go to Joe's House of Blues. We having a good time and that day we went home and had a good day.

Now, 1997, I'm about to make a transition to move out of the hotel and we knew I had to get moving to something nice. So, I had to go out and look for some nice. So, we found a place and they was just fixing on it day to day. I get a call from my father. He saying he had to go to the hospital. So, they kept him. And he was telling me about certain things and I was kind of feeling kind of sad. And he was telling me to bring him Milky Way because he liked the candy bars every night. Then I was telling him, dad, you coming home. And I guess I told my dad that you ain't even had to go to the hospital, you could've just stayed home. And just like I just said, it wasn't that serious. So, they told me it was serious. So, I didn't really think none of it. I was like, dad, you'll be home. So, a day or two went past, he was still there. And I get a call, my father passed away. Oh my god! A part of me losing my father like I didn't have nobody now. I was so hurt.

I lost my dad. He meant world to me. And so now, we got to make preparations to bury him. He got another side of family. I had two brothers, two half-brothers and a half-sister. My father had another set of kids. So, we all get together. And it was real sad. I was real hurt. I lost my old man. I didn't know what to do. But I was strong. I was just more hurt inside. I just ask God to take care of me because he prepared me. My father passed at 71 years old. So, I just look at it and my father lived a good, long-term lifestyle. And during his life, he was a veteran, he was in the Navy, very intelligent. I loved my dad. I used to sleep with my dad at times when I was out there doing drugs and he used to tell me to get myself together. And I used to just say, I'm gonna do the right thing. And a lot of things just came to me. I used to cut my father's toe nails. I really loved my dad, like, he hurted me but I moved on.

CHAPTER 25

So, later on that day, me and my brother, we get ready to go out. We go to the Park Avenue in East Cleveland. We go there and it was a little place at that time. I just wanted to go dancing. Me and him both wanted to do our little thing, go out and have some fun. And I had a good time, no fights, no nothing, it jumped off, it was just a cool day. Most of the times, fights jump off in East Cleveland. But didn't happen, transpired. So, we had a little fun and we went our separate ways. So, I go home, kick back with my girl, wait for the next day and go to work. I'm working at Bob Big Boys Out, Euclid, Babbit Road. Later that day, a couple of the OGs came in and they ordered some food. They gave a confirmation back of the house, which is me. They liked the food. They gave me a $100 tip which I appreciated. It makes me feel that I can touch people's stomachs and they taste good. So, I felt good out doing my thing. I got home, get changed, tell my girl, let's go out and celebrate a little bit. So, we go to Joe's House of Blues. We having a good time and that day we went home and had a good day.

Now, 1997, I'm about to make a transition to move out of the hotel and we knew I had to get moving to something nice. So, I had to go out and look for some nice. So, we found a place and they was just fixing on it day to day. I get a call from my father. He saying he had to go to the hospital. So, they kept him. And he was telling me about certain things and I was kind of feeling kind of sad. And he was telling me to bring him Milky Way because he liked the candy bars every night. Then I was telling him, dad, you coming home. And I guess I told my dad that you ain't even had to go to the hospital, you could've just stayed home. And just like I just said, it wasn't that serious. So, they told me it was serious. So, I didn't really think none of it. I was like, dad, you'll be home. So, a day or two went past, he was still there. And I get a call, my father passed away. Oh my god! A part of me losing my father like I didn't have nobody now. I was so hurt.

I lost my dad. He meant world to me. And so now, we got to make preparations to bury him. He got another side of family. I had two brothers, two half-brothers and a half-sister. My father had another set of kids. So, we all get together. And it was real sad. I was real hurt. I lost my old man. I didn't know what to do. But I was strong. I was just more hurt inside. I just ask God to take care of me because he prepared me. My father passed at 71 years old. So, I just look at it and my father lived a good, long-term lifestyle. And during his life, he was a veteran, he was in the Navy, very intelligent. I loved my dad. I used to sleep with my dad at times when I was out there doing drugs and he used to tell me to get myself together. And I used to just say, I'm gonna do the right thing. And a lot of things just came to me. I used to cut my father's toe nails. I really loved my dad, like, he hurted me but I moved on.

CHAPTER 26

I began going to church since the church is like a hospital. You get sick, it's time to go in. That's the way I look at it. I kind of had the faith and the courage and the motivation into spirituality. But I guess you get tested when you get out of church because you can know the devil or the demons that come at you and see how strong you are. I always kept my guards up and try to fight the situation what I'm dealing with. It was hard but I still have my ups and downs and I'm only human. So, I challenge some of my desires to stay focused. It was a hard task. But I utilize my time on some positive stuff to keep myself going such as working out and doing a little sports, boxing just trying to do a positive thing. But some way it seems to find me somehow. And I just didn't have an answer for it. I could find it in my girlfriend, certain things. She was intelligent and the way she used to always try to correct me by using my words to educate me a lot. And that's why I liked about her because she did really educate me on certain levels. I was just still hard headed. I was just a hard headed guy. You could tell me something and I'd soak it in, it'd be in my head but I just still do something the opposite. I didn't understand that and I couldn't question myself but I just did certain things. I am maintained because I was a cut from a different cloth type of guy. I wasn't an introvert or nothing like that. I was just a guy, was outgoing, observing and I played my position when I'm in the streets. I did what I wanted to do on certain levels. And like I say, I was just trying to get better but I kept going backwards.

CHAPTER 27

What I mean about going backwards, I'll be sober for a year and then I relapse and going to bench for a year. And that disease or drugs, it stays in your body, it recalls. I couldn't fight it and I tried to fight it and it kept calling me. But I realized one thing. I said one day, God let me live. I'm gonna overcome this. So, I thought I was overcoming some of the addiction. But now, it got to a point that me and my girlfriend was getting high together. And that was the worst kind of girlfriend and boyfriend getting high. And we used to argue and get into it. So, one day we got into it and the police came and they ran both of our names in. Come find out, my girl had a warrant but she didn't know nothing about. So, they take her to jail. She had to do time. So, she did six months. She go to Marysville and do two months there and then she got shipped to the pre-release building in Cleveland, Ohio, Downtown, Orange where spent the rest of her time. I needed a break because it was time to get myself together while she was gone. So, I'm getting real money. I'm getting my stuff together. I'm getting money now. So, my back against the wall. So, I stopped getting high and started to get money.

Now I'm in the street, hitting licks. And I'm doing the white-collar crime, doing cheques and all that type of stuff. So, now I'm taking care of my girl. She getting her stuff together, getting clean, getting her stuff together. And In 1998, I moved to a nice place. It was a house, a two-family. I take it downstairs. It had two bedrooms. It was 152nd in the

Collingwood area. It was like next to Collingwood High School. Nice house! And it's called a savage village at that time. So now, I buy me a new truck. I get about $50,000; I go buy me a nice truck. I spend about $15,000 on the truck and then push my crib out. And I'm doing my thing. I'm making sure her money on the books was straight. And so, when she come home, she has something to come home to. Later on, that summer in 1998, she came home. I went down there and picked her up, gave her some money. She still had money for what I sent her. And I took her shopping. And I had a couple outfits for her anyway because I sold clothes but I wanted to take her shopping to make her feel good. She was happy to get home and be with me again. So, now me and her on this sober trade again, so we doing our thing.

Chapter 28

After picking my girl up from the pre-release place, she was very happy to see me and I was very happy to see her. I have brought the truck, Isuzu Rodeo with the Mickey Thompson's on there, fully loaded and it was money green. She was impressed when she seen the truck. She started smiling and I was smiling at her because she got herself together, looking good and what not. And I took her shopping and I took it to the crib. I had a surprise there because I had plush the house out, fish tank and it's the golden mirror tables. Plus, it was real nice. I mean, I was into the Italian furniture and she just knew that by me just being a fly guy that dressed, she knew I had good taste and stuff. So, I've got that from my mom. Because I feel like I was a home decorator. So, I did everything myself. So, she came in and seen everything. She smiled and I loved seeing the smile on her face. So, we get adjusted at the place. Our new place was 152nd Ivanhoe in the Collingwood area. It was like the back cave. That's what I call it because it was off in the cut. I call it the back cave because everybody who knew me and my family said I was a low-key exclusive and I've always been like that to her all the time. But to make a long story short, I had a better surprise for her. I told her, we was going out of town.

I take her to New York which I booked an Amtrak to because she never rode the train. So, I feel like it would be romantic for me and her. She was God's creation just exploring and looking at the land and the trees to make us think and feel good about ourselves because I always wanted to do it and I did it. So, I didn't hesitate about doing something that I wanted to do. I just did it. And I got to New York. We stayed across the street from Madison Square Garden, the hotel. And I took her shopping again. I did my little shopping, went to the Garment District where I get my clothes and the stuff. We stayed there three days and come back home and travelled back home. And she loved everything and I enjoyed everything. And by that time, I started doing my little hustle again and I kind of got out of the white-collar crime stuff. I just started back to my clothes. When I was on a mission by myself and my girl came home, I had to change my direction of getting on my feet. So, now it's in a winter. Winter come. So, I get the urge again. I'm about to turn to 1999. I get the urge again. I go back into this level of getting high again but not with my girl. I'm just doing my thing on the low-key side; it's supposed to be low-key because I couldn't really drink. When I drink, I couldn't control my alcohol. So, I needed something to bring me down so I end up getting high, ausing it again.

CHAPTER 29

It got to the point that I was abusing it. It got worse. So now, I'm getting high and my sister's son, my nephew, I'm banned out from him now. I mean, he was kind of skeptical about selling it but a hustler can always be a hustler. But we were family. e didn't really like doing it but he sold me dope. And I think I got so high that it made him mad that he flipped on me. He gave me some bull shit dope and we got into it; we were kinda go to blows. So, I was spending money with him. So, I'm just telling him that shit wasn't no good and all this and that and I was spending my money. So, we get into a heated argument and we get to wrestling, one of punches strong. So, I say, fucking get the fuck out my house, go head on. I had money in my socks, money in my pocket. You know what I'm saying? I was just on a mission getting high because I just felt like I wanted to take myself out, like really kill myself really because I didn't give a fuck. So, he pulled a gun out on me and say, you don't give a fuck, nigga, I'm anyway just take your life for you. And I say, you feel like that, pull the trigger. He pulled the trigger and the clip jammed. It jammed, just like that because it wasn't meant for me to die.

And that was my nephew. He wasn't meant for my nephew to kill his uncle. He was just hurt. And I was hurt. You know, I felt some kind of way. He felt some kind of way. He told my sister about the situation. Well, nothing she could do because I'm a grown man and he is a grown man. And I just kind of like Wade was, just didn't give her fuck about myself no more. Because I guess at that time, I let myself go because all the stuff that I was thinking and held on, it came back in front of me. And it's just, I guess, about my daughter, my father, my mother, my sister, all this thinking and it wasn't nothing but the devil. I'm saying and think like that because I was abusing. So, I finally brushed it off and got myself together the next couple of days. And then I thought about the things that would have happened. And I was hurt, he was hurt. I forgave him because I loved him and he loved his uncle. Because I was like a role model to him as an uncle because he stayed up under me and he was really disappointed. Like I just said, I had to get myself together because I was hurting a lot of people in my family, especially my kids were young and they really didn't know. If they would have knew, it would have tore them apart. And I had to start thinking what I'm doing to myself. So, I had to slow down and get myself together. So now, I'm getting myself together one day at a time.

CHAPTER 30

As I get myself together, I'm working out, getting back in shape mentally and physically and spiritually. And my girl was giving me a little therapy, just helping me overcome a lot of obstacles because she'd been through the war path with me at the time of getting high. And she was embracing me to believe in myself more because she was really in my corner when nobody else was because we've been through the drug pandemic. So, she understood me more. So, that's how me and her continued our relationship because we was just fighting. And I was fighting these demons, not by myself but a person that cared. So, that kinda like helped me put me back together. And as me detoxing, getting myself together, I didn't go to no treatment or nothing. I just did things on my own. So, now as I detox and stuff like that, I'm getting myself together inside. Not the outside, the inside because I know what the outside is. Like, you look in the mirror, you see yourself, you know what you gotta do. So, I did my homework about myself. And in 2000, me and my girl, we went our separate ways because I had to find myself. So, I met another young lady. She was in a nursing field and very attractive, no younger than me though, couple years younger than me. But she didn't know nothing about my past but like I just say, eventually I had to tell her little things about me. Because I wanted her to know because she really started digging me.

So, I'm staying in Cleveland Heights now. She staying on 105th and Lee and we getting dated. And I'm working at Jillian's, where they shoot pool ads. I'm a cook at Jillian's. So, and I'm working at the Cafe Dior also. I had two jobs. I'm cook in a restaurant on Coventry. It was an Italian restaurant at that time. And, I am doing my thing on that as I proceed with my cooking thing because that was my passion. And me and the girls hit it off but there was something about her that turned me on and something about her that turned me off. And what I mean by that was I started to learn that she was possessive about certain things. She had a lot of insecurities and I think of the insecurities that she was immature and certain things like, we would go out together and eat and people would look at us as a couple and when you were as the couple, women would look at you and flirt. And I look at a woman and I'm a flirt, makes me feel good. You know what I'm saying. I ain't flirting back but compliments makes me feel good. It builds me up because she really don't know that I was at my lowest when I was a drug addict. And I know how that insecurity feels, so it makes me feel good. So, it kept my stamina boosted up like I feel good about myself.

So, we had a strong relationship at one time. She had two kids. And we was getting together and I was still with my other girlfriend. Like I just said, I said to overcome these drugs, I'm gonna start dating women, other women. Like really that was my thing, dating other women and having multiple women. So, I used that as a quest as me getting high no more. So, I would have a couple girlfriends. And make a long story short, I wasn't that good at having a couple girlfriends. I thought I was just doing something to get an understanding with myself. I liked the both of them and I had to be at two places at once. It was kind of hard. Sometimes I drop the ball and sometimes I fumble the ball. I drop the ball without even doing what I'm doing but when I throw the ball I get caught up. So now, I get caught up in my lies because I'm cheating two women. And me and my girlfriend, we really got in a heated argument. And I left the house. I went over to my other girlfriend's house and spent the night. Because I really didn't care no more. I was like, the support that my girl helped me through and the support that I was looking for, it wasn't good enough. So, I lived and I learned from that experience.

Chapter 31

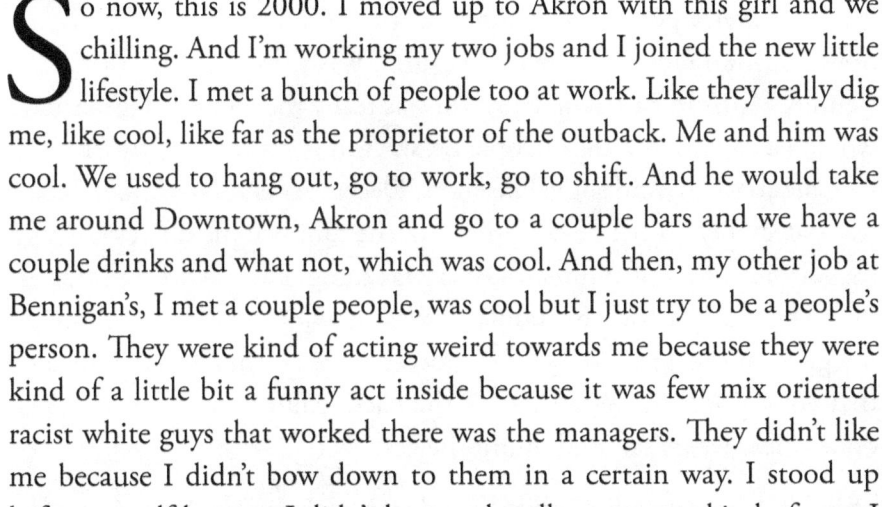

So now, this is 2000. I moved up to Akron with this girl and we chilling. And I'm working my two jobs and I joined the new little lifestyle. I met a bunch of people too at work. Like they really dig me, like cool, like far as the proprietor of the outback. Me and him was cool. We used to hang out, go to work, go to shift. And he would take me around Downtown, Akron and go to a couple bars and we have a couple drinks and what not, which was cool. And then, my other job at Bennigan's, I met a couple people, was cool but I just try to be a people's person. They were kind of acting weird towards me because they were kind of a little bit a funny act inside because it was few mix oriented racist white guys that worked there was the managers. They didn't like me because I didn't bow down to them in a certain way. I stood up before myself because I didn't let people talk to me any kind of way. I knew what I had to do. Again, I just had another job to fall on, so that what's kind of lightweight was more not intimidating. But I didn't have to kiss their ass like, I ain't have another income.

So now, me and my girl and her kids, I go to church and Akron and get baptized. I get baptized in August, 2000. I go into church faithfully every Sunday. It was like a light cross from a walkway of where I was living in a Wilberth apartments. The name of the church was St. John's. Nice church and the minister, he was from the south where my parents come from, Alabama. So, he gave a good sermon all the time. Like I just said, I got baptized in 2000 and I made my girl and her kids get baptized. I was doing something positive because I'm trying to change my little lifestyle. I'm feeling good, living good and doing my thing. And now we doing fun adventures. She used to have a little escort with a stick and I never could drive a stick but that turned me on how she used to drive a stick like she was like a a car race driver. Like we got where we was going and also in reserve gas.

So, she was very intelligent too, but I got to say, she had a lot of immature qualities about herself. But I did my part, like, as a man helping out, doing work and two jobs and bringing that bread and butter home. And we would go shopping and for the kids and for ourselves and we hit it off pretty good. But it came to a time, me and her had a father now. So, she'd take me to work because I was working at Outback and Benn A Chin's in Fairlawn. Fairlawn was really the nicest neighborhood where I'd say middle class people be at. And it was in the winter, she'd take me to work. And some like about December and November. No, it was November. I can't never forget. So, she dropped me off at work and we got into a heat of argument. And next thing, I'm at work and I didn't know how to get back for home. It was snowing real bad. And one of my guys on the line said, hey D, man, come here. And he was like, ain't that your girl? And we by, like, in the back, you can look out the back door where we go out and dump the garbage.

This bitch brings my clothes and dump over by the dumpster. She brought all my clothes out because me and her had an argument and put my stuff out. So, basically when we had an argument, she wanted me out of her apartment. So, I said, wow. So, I didn't know nobody, no place to go. And so, now I'm really upset and trying to call her and she not answering the phone and nothing like that. So, I'm like, wow, I'm on my own. I can go back to Cleveland but I did not want to go back to Cleveland. I kind of liked it up here in Akron. So, you know, Fairlawn was a nice variety of neighborhoods that I can chill. So, at the end of my shift, the guy said, where you going, D? I said, man, take me back, take me home. So, she wouldn't let me in. I get there and it's cold and the guy dropped me off. She wouldn't let me in. So, I called the police. I had to call police on her and tell her, I just get out of work and I've been living with this girl for almost six months. She can't evict me or whatever because I know it's a project but I've been living here and me and her been together. And I ain't got no place to go and it's cold outside.

So, and make a long story short, they let me in. She let me in the apartment and I was so heated that we still was arguing about something I said and something she didn't like. Because I know I got a foxy mouth and she got one. But I know I always know how to verbal abuse because I was always verbal abusive with my mom. She know how to use that tongue to hurt my feelings and I just told her you mess with the wrong person when it comes down to verbal abuse because I can come back and hurt your feelings. So that did, that's what did it make me and her go to the point of she put me out because she didn't like what I said. So, I spent the night, stayed there. The next day, I go to my church that we got baptized at and talked to my pastor. Pastor told me if you're really serious about starting over, it starts right here. So, he prayed over me. And one of the deacons took me in and gave me a ride. He asked me how much money did I have? I said, I got a few hundred dollars to get me through or what not. But I ain't got enough to stay in no hotel till I get on my feet. So, making a long story short, he take me to the shelter. He said, if you really serious about getting your life together, you have to start right here. And this way you determine if you want to go up or go back to where you was at.

So, I went to the Akron in the Shelter, City Mission in Akron was downtown in Akron. So, I stayed there. It was hell but I went through it. I stayed there and go to work from there. So, I kept my clothes over the Deacon house and I took what I needed just to go to work because I'm around people, homeless people like myself at that time and people been on the streets doing drugs and messed up. It was a hell of an experience for me though but it brought a lot of things to my eyes to make me understand what goes up can come down but you can come back up if you believe in yourself. So, now you got to every meal, you got to go to church in the shelter. And that's how they had it, like every time they feed you, we go to church whatever, go to the classes but like I didn't. I worked, so I really at least eat breakfast and then get ready for work. And I used to catch the number two auditing bus to work. It takes me all the way down to Fairlawn. So, one day, I left early because I said I can't live in this shelter. So, all the hotels around there where I worked there because where I worked there, was by the freeway. Benn A Chin's and Outback was by the freeway.

So, they had a little shopping plaza where in Fairlawn where it was so nice. So, it motivated me because I just seen the middle class and the ones who was in a better shape than me. It kind of motivated me to do better. So, I told my deacon that I can't stay in a shelter no more. I gotta go find me a hotel to stay at. So, we go to the Super 8 motel in Fairlawn. And I had my bag. So, I said, I'm gonna make it happen. If it's meant for me, I'm gonna just pay because I'm close to my job. So, I'm gonna work. I got to say, I got a lot of good days. So, I worked my hand with the owner. He was a foreign guy, like a Arab or Indian. Make a long story short, I had my certificate in my hand. But I, telling him, I'm God's child and I'm into the spirituality. I'm trying to get myself together and I explained to him my story that my girl put me out and I like it in Akron and I am not going back. I just want to go to work. But here, can you work with me? I could pay monthly. He hear me out, he heard my story. And he say, I'll charge you $600 a month. So, I said that's fine. He said, can you afford it? I said, yes, I can afford it. So, I gave him $600 right off the top. Dang. I tell my deacon that he can go head on. I'm good and I appreciate you supporting me and help me through my tough times. So now, we're doing our thing.

Chapter 32

So now, I'm at the hotel. I got a nice room with a little kitchen in it and couch. Real nice, elegant, convenient for me. It's really like a studio apartment. I was very happy. So, I was determined to go to the top and get on my feet. Because I didn't give up. So, I sit down and rest and get ready for the next day to go to work. My day job at Benn A Chin's in the morning then I go to my second job at night at Outback which was across the street. I'm feeling good about myself but I'm still kind of lightweight mad because I wanted to get revenge. But I'm bigger than that. So, I just say, my revenge is going to be my success, that's the way I'm thinking. Because I let a female take me out of my element by moving in, she was really crazy about her brother. But like I said, she was on some bullshit. So now I'm at work. My boss called me in the office and say, you got a phone call. So, I'm thinking, who the hell would call me? It's this girl. She wanted to see that I quit my job and still there. So, I'm like, answer the phone. Then I talked to her, like, what do you want? She ain't got shit to say. I'm like, don't call this job no more and I hung up. And I just hope she ain't come up here and try to you fuck with me thinking that I'm gonna come back. She thought I was gonna go back to Cleaveland basically. But I am a survivor. You can put me anywhere; I know how to survive.

So now, I am getting off my work, on my way back to the hotel because I had to. It was like a walk, a nice little walk. You can see my hotel from the job but I had to walk. I had to walk on the freeway to go to the hotel but I had no problem with that. So now, I get in, sit back, gave me some rest. And I was off on both jobs the next day. So, I'm just chilling in my room and the housekeeping lady knock on the door and said you want your room cleaned? I'm like, yeah you can clean it but she was telling me I had to step out for you to clean it because she's not allowed to clean. I'm like, ain't no problem. So, I kept my room clean myself. I said all you can do is just really give me the vacuum cleaner. I could vacuum. You ain't got to do much. She was persistent in the vacuum. And the lady was a Jamaican lady, nice dark skin, thick little bra, had a fat ass. I'm like, say something to her. I mean she smile and I said, damn! where you come from? Because she had a nice body. And she responded back and said she just come home from a joint. I'm like, wow! She stay in the halfway house down in Akron, at an oriental house in Akron.

She said she did time. She said she did, like, about five years. I said what you do? She said well, I went to jail for this guy that I love and we got pulled over. And he had a kilo in his car of cocaine. I do the time. We both do the time. I said, you are a stand-up woman. She was talking in Jamaican accent. It was really attractive to me a little bit because she was good with her words. She knew a lot of English. And she asked me a question. She said, do I have a woman? I said, no, I got no woman. I thew a little front on it. I am like, I have just opened up these two restaurants across the street over there. And I just had to come and stay here for a while. So, she's like, oh. And she, basically she was saying she wanted to fuck me. And I'm like, wow! She said, I ain't had no sex in five years and I want some. And I'm like, for real? I'm like, Okay. She said, you got a condom? I can get one because there's stores right there, whole full little closet with it and whatever, that's why I go out and get one. So, she said, I get off at four, I knock on your door, one knock, you know it's me. I said, okay.

And by that time, it's about like 2.30 in the afternoon. So, I'm like, wow! I'm about to hit this. And 4 o'clock came around. She knocked on the door. She was real serious and ain't waste no time. She just told me to take off everything and let's to it. And I'm like, say less. I pulled my clothes. She laid on the bed and I got up in there. I went to work. After we were finished, she went away. I went my way. I'm at my hotel but I'm like, I'm about to go get me some tea or whatever. If you just want to come by sometimes, if I'm here, just knock on my door. I wish they got a key, so they could come in. So, I was kind of near about that looking Jamaican with a nice ass, nice titties. But now she, she read the word. Because there's more women in housekeeping to do the room. So, when I go out my room for work or go get some ice, I see that housekeeping ladies and they, like, in the laundry room talking about me. So, I feel like I'm the shit now. Like this other girl, she was bad. She was going to oriental house too because I think, like, basically they from oriental house, work at the hotel trying to get on their feet. So, they then would go back and doing something, like, productive.

So, I was hollering this sister. She was a mix. She was half black and half Indian. She was pretty. But I don't know what she went jail for but I didn't really get into it while asking her a thing. So, she's flirting with me. She would come and do my room time to time and I'm having a good time. So, she asked me., can I come over and kick it with you before I go back to the halfway house? I said, yeah. She said, what day is you off? I said, I am off on Thursdays and Fridays. She was like, cool. She said, I want to get with you because I heard you put it down. And I'm like, I don't know what you are talking about. I'm playing along, I heard about. So, she really wanted to have sex with me. I'm like today must be my lucky day for me leaving this girl and get on my feet and have sex with different women. That was up my alley. I got the bachelor spot at the hotel. I'm feeling good about myself. So' I ended up busting her down. And it was on. I kept everything discreet because the owner didn't know nothing about it. They kept it discreet. So, when I was off there, I would have sex with this Jamaican one day and have sex with the Indian girl, this mix breed the next day. And I was having fun. I was living my best life. So, now time fly. So, the owner came to me and say, well, when summertime come, I get a lot of business. And I have to go up on your rate from $600 to $800 because I can't, people come from out of town like you just say, I'm right by the freeway and people need his rooms. So, I told him no problem. I will give you the eight. So, I stayed there at least about six months and I had a good run when I stayed in the six months. So, now it's going to 2001. It's going back to the autumn season. So, now I'm doing my thing.

CHAPTER 33

Now, I went to time in autumn season, my hotel, my stay in there is about to expire. So now, I have to make the decision where I am gonna move to. So, what I do is, go back and forth to Cleveland which I didn't want to because I was on a journey on goals. I made a setback to go back to Cleveland but I had to. Because like I say, I wanted to start off in Akron but I really didn't have a vehicle. So, to get around, I was stacking my money but I was still going through a lot of things. I would go back to Cleveland on my off days and I stayed at my sister's house. She stayed out in Euclid, Ohio. I think I was there; I think her son was getting married, my nephew. So, they had a reception on 93rd in Cleveland. And I went to the reception and met his wife's cousin. She digging me because I'm dressed. And impressed with her. She was nice looking and she had big titties that would really turn me on too, the yellow bone. So, I get with her, get her number. We started hooking up. And she came to visit me at the hotel out in Akron. She really dig me. So, she came way out to Akron. I said, it is on. So, we started kicking it and one thing led to another, we had sex. I put it down and she was locked in with me, I just told her. She understood that where I was going and my goal was. So, she was on the team with me. So, now I can lock her in or just keep her for a spare.

So, I end up running into my ex-girlfriend, the one I've been with for a long time, was in recovery with me. We used to get high together, put it like that. And she had something about her, I still loved her. I was still in love with her. She had these hooks into me that I really loved. I don't care how many other women I dealt with; I always loved her out of all of them. So, her mama owned an apartment building on Superior Hill. She was staying in one of her apartments and she just cleaned apartments and whatever. So, her mama had some property and what not. So, I am back to juggling two women again. The same girl I left, the girl that I moved to Akron with. Now I'm back with the girl, my ex. But now I got another little side chick on the side dealing with her. So, I end up, making long story short, I end up smashing my ex. We had sex. We made love. We ain't had sex, we made love. Put it like that. She knew I was not all into her like I used to be because she knew my journey but she knew me and she was trying to win me back. But I was still dating my nephew's wife's cousin. So, now I am still going back and forth to Cleveland, from Akron to Cleveland. Because I am still doing my thing, working. So, I stopped.

CHAPTER 34

It's 2002 now. I made a transition to move back to Cleveland. I got a transfer from the Outback in Fairlawn to Lyndhurst. So, I am working there and I moved also back to a hotel, a charter house. So, now I'm back in Cleveland. And now I am doing another job. It's to attempt service working at Dirt Devil. I gotta do what I had to do just to keep myself on the right track. I was doing good for a couple months working two jobs but I started to get burnt out, so I had to let the Dirt Devil job go. I stayed there for about four months. And I'm working in Outback Steakhouse. At the process of that time, I meet a young lady at Dirt Devil Factory. And she used to give me a hard time on the assembly line. And I was just thinking like, why this lady always keep messing with me and what not. And come find out I knew she liked me because the line would stop and she would always say something to me like, it's my fault but it wasn't. She was nice looking. She was like a WNBA player. She was tall, nice boobs, nice booty, it looked like she worked out, nice thighs and everything, had anita baker haircut. And she had drove a nice look Honda like the fast and fury cars made like that and she dated white boys in that place at Dirt Devil.

She wasn't interested in brothers. But knowing me, I kind of changed the whole thing around, I changed the game. Because I knew that when, as time went on, we would get into an argument. And I met a couple of guys there that worked with, it was cool and we started hanging out. And so, make a long story short, me and her got into an argument and

I blew down on her and asked her, what is it? You got something against me because it seemed like you always have something to say? She kind of blew me off and I kind of, felt rejected. So, I had to use a different strategy, a different approach. So, I kind of, fell back and just ignored it because I felt like I was stupid to her level being argumental and she would still go at me. And I kind of, knew that she liked me and the ladies on the line and the people in the place knew that she liked me. So, she was messing with these white dudes in the place. He was a nice-looking white dude with the little ponytail and what not and he was like a half breed. But I ain't care about no other dog, no other guy. So, me and my guy got into it about I can't knock her off. I am like, man, I'm trying to get on my feet. I ain't stuck in that lady. But I did like her because I like competition. That's what made me like her.

So, I end up knocking her off. So, I told her like, let's go out and have a drink. And we ain't got to be always be beefing at each other. Can we go out and have a drink? So, I persuaded her to go out and have a drink. That's all she wrote. We go to this club called For You To Be. It's on 260th on Euclid. It's like not too far from where we work at. So, me and one of my guys who work with me and her, we all go there and have a couple of drinks and what not. And she get a buzz on. We get to dancing. So, we were about to leave and she's like, can you do me a favor, go and get a six pack of Heinekens? And I say, okay. And she said, and also grab a rubber. I'm like, wow, for real? So, I am like, say less. So, I did that. And we go back to my spot. It was all she wrote. I tore that ass up. So, from there on, she digging me and she picking me up from work and dropping me off. At the time, I ain't had no vehicle but one of the guys, I used to ride with to work, he would come and swoop me up because it was like I went too far from the job. So, it was just like one straight shot. She doing it now. So, I'm locked in. We ain't got together. We just had sex and then she is liking me and then we was cool at the same time. We kept our distance; we kept a professional when we was at work. But a lot of people kind of, started knowing down the stretch because on our break, we had meet up and she'll go sit in her car and I go holler at the guys that I work with. And the word is spreading. So, that right there happened. And she had her stuff together. She was also in the service at one time. So, she had to get a check in. She had her own house. She stayed on a 109th in St. Clair and she was well known around that neighborhood.

I came over to the house a couple of times but I really wasn't into her like that. Because like I say, I was just being a man and just doing what anybody else would do, see something nice, you want it, you get it. So that relationship didn't last too long. So, now I stayed there like about six months. And I quit that job. Well, I didn't quit. I guess there come time to get hard in, the Dirt Devil, they had to move to Minner. So, their contract with that building had expired. So, I wouldn't want to go away out of Minner because I didn't have no transportation and I wasn't going to be raving and hurting. So, I just left that job alone and I just stayed with Outback which I was getting burnt out. So that's me and her, kind of like, went our separate ways. So now, one of my friends I grew up with let me get one of his Toyota Land Cruisers. No, a Toyota 4runner. So, with the Mickey Thompson's and the crash bars on it, nice little system. So, we are like family. I was like his older brother. So, he let me use it, use the truck. You know what I'm saying? He barely, like, really gave it to me. And I'm getting around. So, now I got some wheels and I guess I end up stumbling across my ex-girlfriend who was, her mama had owned an apartment building on Superior Hill.

So, we end up linking up. And I end up spending the night over there. And I really started, I moved in. I moved in with her for about six months. So, now I am working at Outback and I'm not too far from my job. And I come home and the area that I lived on Superior Hill, up by Forest Hill, it was kinda. drug-infested. Her building where she stayed at, everybody that stayed around that bit from East Cleveland, whatever and Cleveland Heights on the border, it was a gang. It was territorial. They was called the Hilltop and they was well known around there. So, I see myself start to get these urges again. And I'm doing my thing, working to one day, I relapsed. That's what all she wrote. And so, I really was like a closet smoker. So, now it got to the point, it was starting to get worse. I didn't bring my ex-girlfriend into it because she was in recovery. I ain't wanna tear her down. So, I see myself getting worse. So, me and her went our separate ways. So, now I left.

CHAPTER 35

2003 and 2004, I end up going to a comedy club in a hotel I was staying at. Me and my cousin and his wife and another friend he had, she wanted me to meet. She worked at the post office. And I came down to the comedy club. They was all sitting down, having a good time. I think at that time, Damon Williams was the comedian. I had on a gator print outfit. It was black and gold with the silk, in black gold shoes. I was sitting down and Damon Williams made a joke at our table. He picked on me. So, he asked me to stand up and show my outfit off. So, he began laughing, cracking on me with my outfit. And the girl at the table that I was sitting with was laughing. My cousin, his wife was laughing at me. So, I thought it was funny because we were at a comedy club and I got a little roasted. So, I had a good time. And the young lady that I met from the post office, we end up going back to my room, talking. She was nice too. She had a nice body, thick. And I kind of dig there. I'm just taking my time with this one. So, we just talk, drunk a little wine and what not. I better, gave her a kiss on the cheek and then we hooked up the next day. The next day she came over. We went to Perkins to have lunch, talking, getting to know each other.

So, we came back to my hotel. We had sex. And that's all she wrote from there. So, she spoiled me, showing me a good time. And she was into me. I was into her. I was trying to still work on myself at the same time. So, I guess we start seeing each other more and more and during the summer of 2003, we end up hooking up, going out, having fun. At this time, I'm working at shooters in The Flats, not shooters, I mean Fagan's in The Flats. We kicking it down in The Flats having a good time. And, we digging each other. We holding hands, cuddling and everything. And I'm making her feel real special treating a woman how a woman is supposed to be treated. So, now she come to me with a suggestion, telling me to move in with her. So, now I'm like, for real? You want me to move in with you? She lived in Warrensville. She had her own house and she had a son. Her son was real square, real quiet type young dude at that time. And I ended up moving out of the hotel. She helped me, packed up all my stuff and I moved in with her in Warrensville. So now, we doing our thing. We go to Akron over to a friend house to; that I knew moved in Akron and we went to go see the fireworks. A lot of people were just staring at her because she had a nice body and a little waist. That's what made me get attracted to her. She had a nice body and her personality was real nice. Yeah. I seduced her and she seduced me.

So, we end up making love and I end up getting her pregnant. She told me she was pregnant. I started to see another side of her and it was a mean side. So, I knew it was a test 22 when I moved in with this woman. Most of the time, a woman usually move in with the man. But in my situation, I moved in with her. So, I wasn't saying I was down on my luck. I was just staying in a hotel because I was getting on my feet. And when I moved in with her, she had a plush house. Everything I needed. She liked to cook. I didn't have to worry about nothing. She had a big backyard where I could just sit in the back on the patio and just look at the trees and the grass and drink the wine and sit back and mind my business. And it was very peaceful where she lived at. So, we started having some issues because now that I knew she was pregnant. And when women get pregnant, some of them be nice and some of them be kind of fussy. So, this one here was kind of fussy. So, eventually we start having our fallouts and it got to a point that I moved out and never looked back. So, I kind of, say, well, I don't know if this baby was mine, but I knew it was mine. I was just mad. So now, we're not speaking. And she didn't even tell me nothing about she was in labor or nothing. So, I could see the baby be born. So, now that I heard through the grapevine that I had a daughter. She had a daughter. I had a little girl. She took me downtown, child support and we took a DNA test and then found out It was my daughter.

So, now I just wanted to be in her life now because I wasn't a good father with my three kids that I had. So, I figured I could be a better father to my daughter. It took me a while, to me and her to get along. So, I started going by to see my daughter and hold her. And she was little. I think she was at the time when I finally came around to visit my daughter, she was a couple months old. So, ever since then, I start trying to be more in her life. For being the mother still did get along, I tried to make it right but she was still like, she had some kind of beef with me and I tried to make it right. But I looked over her issues because I did a lot of things to her such as I moved in and got her pregnant which she really didn't want to have no child at the time. By me, that's how I looked at it. But she said that I manipulated her. I was the only guy that moved in her house, that she liked it and got her pregnant. So, some down the stretch, I feel that she kind of disliked me for that. But then, down the stretch was that, when our daughter was born, I think she felt the little more happy. Because she could see a better version of herself between this little girl that we got. So, I end up staying away for a while because me and her ain't get along but I end up coming back to her and try to be a better father because that's what I wanted to do. So, now it's 2004.

CHAPTER 36

2004, now I'm working at Case Western Reserve. I'm cooking as a cook. I work in the second shift position as a cook. And also, I'm living in Cleveland Heights. Me and my kids' mothers, the second baby mother, brother, we still going through our disagreements about me coming around my daughter. And she didn't allow me to do the things she wanted to be done. I can say for myself, I was in a position that I was like an average guy with an average job. I wasn't getting all that street money no more, so I kinda like, it changed my life a little for the best because now I had a daughter, another daughter, to try to be a better father. But I stopped seeing my daughter because me and her weren't getting along. So, I'm just doing me for now, I'm working. And I'm paying child support. I'm trying to get myself back on my feet. It was a slow process but I did it with the progress. I meet another young lady at my job. Now, she was working in the pizza station and I was working the grill. The college students would come in and get their food and stuff.

She would always look at me. She had a dude though, but she wasn't happy. She was very nice looking, very attractive. She had a very sexy appeal about herself. I know she had a lot of guys at her but they say you are not supposed to miss business with pleasure at work. I was like, to say to myself, I got to hire her. She was tall, thick, like one of them down south country girls. So, I start talking to her and asking her questions. She ain't blowing me off. She was very flirtatious but I guess because all the guys and the college students flirted with her and everything. And I thought I couldn't, I didn't have a chance but I ain't give up. I get what I want and I always got what I want to. So, I asked her, can we get together and go out and have a drink or go to dinner. She was like, maybe one day. So, I said, I'm gonna hold you to your word. So, she gave me the spin move, which was cool. And to one day, she probably said, we can go out and meet somewhere.

CHAPTER 37

My new lady friend, I met at work, she finally gave me the opportunity. We can get together and go out. So, we met at Jillian's pool hall in Cleveland Heights. We and a couple of my friends, associates that we met. They also met me up there. They brought a couple lady friends with them also. So, we shooting the conversation with each other and shooting pool and entertaining the ladies at the same time. So, I was waiting on my lady friend to come. She came. And everybody was like wait! looking at her, like, wow! Where you meet her from? So, I'm telling, we work together. And I'm, like, damn! She's nice. I said, I gotta lock her all the way in. So, I just talked with the fellas but I am letting the other ladies get acquainted with her. She was very friendly and the other ladies was very friendly. So, we were shooting pool and we all ordered drinks. We were taking turns ordering rounds. So, the alcohol started to kick in and I started seeing a different side of her. So, she was getting flirtatious with me and whatever. So, we stood around, shoot pool for a couple hours and then we started talking. And one thing led to another, so we ended up going back to my house. And the guys, they went their ways because they had something to do. So, I really wanted to be with her one-on-one and we went back to my house.

We were little tipsy and stuff and I put on some real old school slow jams where I was like saying, you know how to hand dance? And she said a little bit. So, I throw some nice music and we used to dancing and I was teaching her because she wasn't that coordinated but that's my thing. So, I showed her. And then we start slow dancing. And we started kissing and from there on, it was on. We end up getting them draws. And it was all she wrote. I went to my bedroom and I knew what I had to do. So, I locked her all the way in. She was feeling good and she was impressed. But she, like I just say, she still had a guy but he was always gone. He was more of a hustler like I used to be but he took care of his business, he took care of home but she was tired of him. I think they had a kid together. I wasn't stepping on no man's toes or whatever. She was liking me. So, when we got back to work, it was a different approach now. She was smiling at me; I'm smiling at her but we keeping it more professional and being real discreet. She was asking me what I got going on this week. So, I was like, I ain't had nothing really going on. We were just talking.

And after our shift was over, I get a call from my baby's mother too. She saying, I'm throwing our daughter a little birthday party and I want you to come by. I'm like okay, that's fine. You invited me to come by to see our daughter. So, I end up telling the young lady that I work with, did she wanna go to a little thing with me, a little party with me, my daughter's party. And she said yes, she would love to. So, she accepted the invitation and we went to my daughter's party. We pulled up in a 430LX Lexus. At that time that was a brand-new Lexus she had, like, it was a 2004. So, I'm stunned now because I'm riding with her and she is into me. So, I pull up and get out of the car. Everybody was in the backyard. So, we walked to the back and started to approach the backyard. I see my kid's mother's family, they staring us down. And in my mind, I already knew how she felt because she probably thought I couldn't move on and do better. I saw the hatred come out but she didn't say it, I just seen it. But I ignored it.

And my daughter, she was on a trampoline jumping around. She came back and gave me a hug and everything. My daughter gave me a hug. I introduced my lady friend to my kid's mother and family and they was looking at her all kind of crazy, which I didn't care. So, it is what it is.

So, we just stayed for a couple hours. I gave my daughter her present and she was having fun with her little friends. So, me and my kid's mother, we conversated a little bit. We left it like that. So now, I began to get ready to leave because I could feel the people talking smack about me or whatever. So, me and her got out of there. We left. I kissed my daughter and left. So, we end up going to a bar where we can hear music and you can also dance, so we end up doing that. And we started to have a good time because we was laughing and talking and some of the music that she liked it, I liked it and I actually did. You want to dance? So, we end up dancing. And we was having fun. So, she was in all the way into me now.

Chapter 38

2005, me and my daughter, my youngest daughter, me and my kid's mother, we were kind of getting along but we wasn't. But because of our daughter, we worked things out. And she did a lot for my daughter. She really spoiled her. And she brought her a scooter, a spearmint green and white, like an old school scooter, like, back in the day in the 50s, them type of schoolers. It was so unique and cute. So, I charged it up and I told my daughter, let's go ride. She was scared to ride it because she thought she would fall. And I told her I got her, so I told her to get in the front on the scooter and I would ride in the back and I showed her how to ride it and hold the throttle and we would ride through the sunset, through the orange field and maple hikes. And people would honk their horns and mount the scooter because it was one of the old schools, like I said before and me and my daughter would look so cute on it because it was a little one. By me being an adult and having my daughter, the little skinny guy, I fit in right on the scooter, they probably looked at me like I was a little kid but it was my daughter. Me and her was just, at that time, just crumpled up on the scooter and they looked at like, really one person. But they would see her and like I say, people was just giving us two thumbs up and we just ride and just having fun kicking it. And we would ride till we got tired of riding.

So, that was one of our things that we did. And we also used to go to the gym to the YMCA. I would go and work out and my daughter would go swimming. She loved to play in the water. I started her playing in the water to let her swim but she start learning things on her own because I used to just leave her there in the shallow water and she saw the other kids at play. So, she start looking at them and I guess she advanced real good at learning how to swim. And she would sometimes go and she would say, daddy, I want you to see me swim. And I used to say, okay, I watched her swim. I was very proud that she was trying. So, now I had to get in the water with her sometimes and show her and swim because I taught my son how to swim. I might as well teach my baby girl how to swim. She can adapt and learn real quick. After that, she didn't want me around no more for her to swim because she can play with the other kids that was her age. And I was glad that she wanted to do that. So now, we had to do this every day now. We would go, she would go swimming, I would go work out which that I needed to work out to put myself together because it was helping me as a therapy of my mental. I was to a breaking point. I stayed consistent and my mental was really getting strong again with my daughter and myself.

And, afterwards we would go change in the locker room. She would go in the locker room, girls' locker room to change. I was going to men's the locker room. We would meet out. And I'd always meet her out and I'd be waiting for her to come out of the locker room. But for some odd reason, she'd been there a long time. So, I used to have to tell one of the workers to go in there and tell her to come out of there. And I don't know what she's doing because wasn't nobody in there but I kind of figured that she was just playing around in the locker room just being a kid. So, I used to ask her what she was doing. She was like, daddy, I wasn't doing nothing. I was getting dressed. And I was like, are you okay? We would go get something to eat. We would go to a restaurant like BW3's or Chipotle's from a long day of exercise and extremely burnt out. And then we would just talk and we go home. And she would go to bed I would be on my way. I would go home. Sometimes I would spend a night with her because her mother let me sleep in the other guest room and she always wanted to sleep with me. So, at a certain time, she had her own room but she would love to sleep with me all the time. And I really liked that. That really touched my heart.

CHAPTER 39

I would spend a night with my daughter, make sure she's next to me sleep. And I know I gotta get up in the morning, go to work. So, I will tip toe out of there, kiss her on the forehead and get ready to go home and prepare myself for work later on that day. But I always leave because my new girlfriend, she would call me at a certain time in the morning because she worked the first shift. She worked the first shift and she loved to hear my voice and I always talked to her but I would be driving on my way home. She didn't know about me spending a night in my kid's mother house. It was really none of her business or what I did because she lived with her baby's father. So, I was just doing me. And she was insecure at the same time because the type of guy I was, I can get any woman I wanted but I wasn't really on that right now. I'm just trying to find myself and make ends meet to go back to another level. Because now I got a daughter that really needs me and want things that I can provide for her. So, I get home, I get a call from my cousin. He had a plan and we were talking on the phone. He was telling me about his brother in Houston, about the weed. Now there's a drought in Cleveland and we were talking about getting together. So, he come back before I get home and we talked about the weed situation. He said that if I would front him, his brother would front him some pounds. And I'm like, well, the money kind of funny. I'm like, what you talking about?

So, we at that time, we bought four pounds. He put up the money, bought four pounds and his brother fronted us four more, so we had eight pounds. So, he wanted to see how it moved. So, I tell my cousin that by me working at a college, college students smoke weed all the time, so that's not a problem about me moving it but I had to break my ice down. And he also had a hookup and doing a network on the street side. So, we doing our thing now. I work in the college and he work in the street. While I'm at work, so I would sell to the college students and some of the employees that I work with. The word traveled fast because I had good weed and it was a drought so I would have that clientele and the college students. I would let some of them know and give them a tester and they would come back and wanna buy some. So, I'm taking off, the word spread it fast. So now, I'm at work being low key and I would serve food. Because during lunch time they would always come to my station, at the grill station. I would serve them the food and they would tell me what they want. And I always had the weed stashed in my food area and I always had quarter bags so they was buying quarters left and right. And I was like wow! Money started coming in and put a big smile on my face. I'm feeling good. I'm grossing $300-$400 a day. So, now we doing my thing. My cousin, he's out networking in the streets selling ounces.

CHAPTER 40

The weed business is getting good to me now. I'm at the college at Case Western Reserve getting my grind on. I upgraded as far as selling more weed. So, our connect dropped us 18 pounds. I stashed them in my basement because I stayed in a two-family house. I had a place there where I could put it at and it wouldn't smell because I didn't want my neighbor upstairs smelling it when she come down to wash clothes. And I kept a lowkey, low profile. I was a little nervous because at that time I never had that much weed. But they feel good looking at the money. And I can take care of a lot of things such as my bills, about my daughter, nice little things and do things for myself. So, now it's going on 2006, wintertime. So, me and my cousin, we was just talking and we know this was going to come to an end one day. So, we were just talking about how we can expand. So, we came up with a suggestion. Just like we're gonna just sell these 18 pounds and that's it. We cooled on that because we didn't want to catch no case.

So now, we celebrate. We book a flight to go to Vegas to the fight, the boxing match to go see Floyd Mayweather fight. So, we stayed in MGM hotel where the fight was at. And we went to the fight, we had a good time. We rented a car, rolled around on the strip. I was very happy because I'd never been to Vegas. And just to go see a boxing match, I felt like a celebrity. But my cousin showed his other side because he was thought he was the head of the operation. He will envy me because I was still that fly dresser and still doing what I do. So, he will say things to get me upset, try to get me upset and try to hurt my feelings to see what type of guy I was. I didn't pay that no attention. I just feel that on the financial side, he was married and he had a backup plan. And like I said, he thought he was better than me. And I wasn't no competition, I was just being myself, as just trying to hustle and survive.

I don't judge men. And I don't think I'm better than no man. Because I have my no self-esteem about myself that I'm dealing with, just being skinny and financially, not educated on certain things. I just had a lot of street smarts. So now, we're having fun. We stayed in Vegas for about three days. We went shopping, went to the Charleston mall and buy through pieces. I just had to get some souvenirs, like, see but pretty much everything is the same everywhere as far as, getting outfits. But it's hustling the money, so I just splurged a little bit. So, we go back home, get on our flight, catch the red-eye back home and it's back to business. We're still doing our thing on it, on the weed. Me and my new girlfriend, we seeing each other a lot. But I had some issues with myself. I was still letting these demons get the best of me. And what I mean by that, I will make bad decisions, relapsing.

CHAPTER 41

So now I'm smoking Primo cigarettes. I'm not doing that bad but still, the addiction that I had was so strong, the urges come back every six months or every year. I can stay clean for six months or a year but urges always chase me. And I try to just find a solution to these urges. It's a mental thing, really. I didn't need no AA or NA or none of that. I've been through that. Like I just say, it's a mental thing and one day I'm gonna overcome this drug addiction. But I'm fighting and it get the best of me. And now ain't nobody know I was abusing but myself. I kept it to a point, I was already a skinny guy but I worked out and stuff like that. And I dressed and kept myself groomed but it was just a point in me knowing that I'm using. And I'm real discreet about it because I will be a late night creep when I would just be by myself. When I go out in the streets and get drugs, not a lot of drugs, even though. I sold drugs. I just know where to go but I would disguise myself for people who couldn't recognize me. I would wear all black at night time. It was crazy but it is what it is when you had addictions.

And then I do a chuckle and hide back to working and hustling in my little weed and therefore I didn't let it get out of hand. I kept it. Well, it didn't affect me like far as getting my money and just being worse than what it was. Because all the years that I did drugs, I was still bad but I had some kind of control over it a little bit. And I think those were my stages that I was just getting tired of it. So now, me and my new girlfriend, she didn't know nothing about it. Me and her spent time, she would come over and spend half the whole day with me and she would go home. We would go out and hang out. I'd do things with my kids, my two oldest daughters and we'll have fun. And my youngest daughter, them three days was really important to me. I really love my daughters but I knew that I was hurting myself and they didn't understand because they was young and I kept it real discreet from them. Because I was a good dad but I was also a bad dad because I was abusing my body. I just had to learn a hard way. So now, we would hang out and do things. I've always been more family-oriented with my kids. We do a good things.

CHAPTER 42

So now, me and my new girlfriend get more involved with each other. Summer come, it's midsummer. The college is out on summer break. They go home so we get a little break and come back in September. Me and her spending more time together, we doing little things, going to the gym and to the movies and swimming, all that type of stuff. And also, I spend time with my daughters. They be on their summer break from school. We'll hang out to like a big family, her daughter and my daughters. And we'll just sit around the house and barbecue and laugh and talk, enjoy each other for the most part. We also go out. Me and my new girlfriend, we'll go have a couple drinks and go dancing. We'd come back home; we'd kick back and make love. And I dig her but then again, I wasn't really all the way into her because she deal with a baby's father. Even though she was my girlfriend, I know she really wanted me to be with me but I didn't have the finances. I mean, I sold weed and it was cool but I only had enough to really survive because I lived in a house, a two-family house and I had to pay my own bills and pay my own way. And I'm a high maintenance, I like the best of fashion and I keep my kids on the fashion side too. So, I really didn't have the money to splurge like that with her. Her baby father took care of her. She wore the best of everything. She had a new Lexus, wore gaiters and furs and all that stuff. That's what I liked it too about her.

But I knew I couldn't have her all the way. But she can have me all the way because I was a one woman's man but I wasn't. Because I just felt like I had to keep my head above water. I can't let no woman play me, with my emotions because I've been through that field before being locked up. So, I kind of, just did me. And she didn't like it but there was nothing she could do about it. She liked my game and she liked my sex game also. So, that was me, that kept her, that kept us together. But then, I kinda came into a mental illness. What I mean by the mental illness, I kinda, like, got depressed and it made me get back into getting high because I these thoughts started coming all the time, the urges and just what do I been through and stuff. It's like, I kind of like messed my life up, really like, far as catching these felonies. So, I felt uncomfortable because I was trying to do better and it seemed like, the more I pushed myself, the more I take ten steps backwards. I didn't understand it because I was trying to do the right thing. I was doing the right thing. And it made me relapse. And when I relapse, I started doing criminal minded stuff such as doing a credit card scam again. And it wasn't because I wanted to get high. It's because that's the way I was. Just, like, the streets kind of made me that way. And I was just trying to escape that life.

So, I got really involved in doing it again. And, I fell deep into it again and when I was getting high, I really didn't care again about nothing. I cared about myself but I didn't because I thought something was wrong with me, like, maybe you need to see a shrink or I was messed up mentally. I couldn't blame my parents or whatever, like, this and that and me doing dumb shit to myself. I just suffered from depression and it took me there and I kinda was hitting licks and trying to please the new girlfriend, buying her things expensive things. And then, me on the other side, I would get high and like I just say, it was just messed up. I just didn't care. It would be discreet but it's just, like I'm just saying, I know what I was doing to myself. But they say you know better, you do better. That ain't always true because I didn't have no mentor or I didn't really go around nobody because the people that I knew, they wanted to see me fall or the people that I got hard way or by myself, I was my worst nightmare. I was my worst enemy. Until I got to a point that I was doing these licks on a credit card scam. I get caught up.

Now it's going in 2008. And I had an Infiniti, a nice Infiniti, the car with the chrome rims on it, sitting on twenties with the little sunroof. I had bought it from a college student at where I worked at, Case Western Reserve. And by this time, I moved out my house and I moved into an apartment building around a corner on Coventry. It was a nice apartment where all the college students hang out. And it was a nice apartment and I started hitting licks. And to one day, I get a call on my phone and it was the police. And they said they had me on camera, me and another lady. And I had the credit cards going in the stores, buying stuff. So, they was like, we looking for you. And I'm like, can you tell him that he won something? That's the scam, they try to run on me and it's like, tell him that he had won something and we were just trying to verify some information we'd like to get from. Can he come out to the police station? And I told them, I played down with them and told them like, I would let him know and I would tell him. Wish they knew it was me because they found my phone number. So, it was just a matter of time for they catch me. So, I ignored it. They was looking for me until they say, well, we can't catch him, so we're going to leave a message. And they say to him that we looking for you, we gonna catch you. So, they used to ride past my apartment but they didn't know which apartment I stayed. They just know my car was parked on the street.

I had a white Infiniti with the sun roof, fully loaded, XJK, with the 20s and chrome on there and they knew I was a fly person. So, I stick out like a sore thumb. So, I stopped driving that car. Nah, I'm catching a bus to work and leave my car parked. So, I may have work one day. The chef came and got me and said I need to talk to you. So, he's like took me in the back office. Yeah, the undercover was there waiting for me. And it's like, I told you I was gonna get you. So, I had a bunch of weed on me, in my stash. I didn't have it on me but I had it stashed somewhere by my grill station. And they arrested me and took me on out of the campus and people was looking like, Oh man, what'd Darrel do? I'm like, oh no! What's going on? I'm saying, they probably for traffic ticket. That's what I'm playing in and I asked them, to undercover, y'all just take me to jail for traffic tickets? They don't need to know my business or whatever. They are like we got you. So, they walked me out and I just told my one of the guys that get that stash, get my bag, my little hustle bag behind the station and give it to my girlfriend, new girlfriend and she'd take care of it. So, by that time they had questioned her and knowing I didn't got her involved. So, a woman gonna be scared, she got more to lose. So, I had to take the rep because I ain't wanted her to be involved because it was me doing the credit card scam. And I was just buying her stuff. She was just with me. So now, I take the fall I end up doing some time and I'm going back to the penitentiary and doing. I do 18 months. I come home in 2011.

CHAPTER 43

2011, I've been released from the penitentiary. I stayed in the halfway house for a month and I started working at an upscale restaurant. And while I was in the halfway house for a little bit of time, I established a relationship with my kid's mother, my youngest daughter's mother. She worked at the post office and she was a good. I mean, she was a good lady. I can say not really bad but we just fall out a lot. Because at that time when I got her pregnant and we kind of rushed into things. So, I think we both knew that. That's why we probably didn't get along but now, so I try to rekindle the relationship and tell her how much I missed her and what not and I can help her out with some of the bills because I'm working and whatever and we can be together. So, she was fine with that. And when I came home, I wanted to see my youngest daughter which I missed a lot. I know I had my other daughter, I missed all of them but I wanted to really see my youngest daughter because me and her had a little bond. And she was young when I went down to penitentiary. So, I just wanted to catch up and be a better father. So now, I'm back in justice and society. And I'm living with my kid's mother. And we're not really not in a relationship. We're just trying to be close to begin a relationship to raise our daughter and go to the next level.

So, we getting along. I'm going to work. She going to work. I'm being a family man. I'm watching my daughter. She will go third shift and I would work morning shift, first shift, rather. So, we bumped heads. And like I just say, when she come home, I would get my daughter dressed for school. She would come home and go to sleep and I would go to work with my daughter. My daughter would sleep with me and I'd get her ready for school. And mother would help me out too because I live with her, so she already know the routine about her getting her together. We didn't sleep together but I slept in the guest room. And my daughter had a room but she slept with me majority of the times. Because she missed me and she feel like she wanted to be up under me. And that was with much love. So, that made me really got attached to her more and more. And I try to sleep with my kid's mother at times or what not. But like I just say, we just took one step at a time, trying to see where relationship go but to me, it feel like it wasn't going like it's supposed to. It wasn't about the sex; it was just about certain things that I wanted and certain things she wanted and we really didn't see eye to eye. Basically, our time frame was off because I worked the first shift and she worked the third shift. And we can't really do nothing that much.

So, we digging each other but it wasn't working. So, time went on. So, I was more like into my daughter because I had a lot of things, I had to think about. Because I really liked my ex-girlfriend, the one that had the baby's father, she lived with and we broke it off because she had met somebody else while I was incarcerated. And I did them 18 months. I thought she was gonna stick in for the long run but like I just say, I get locked up always. I had no support, so it was rocky. I should have known but I had a lot of things to do to evaluate myself to be a better man. So now, since I'm out in society and adapting again making a lot of justice and being a working man and being drug free and which I did stay drug free. I just thought about all the things that I did, so I really had a passion for cooking. So, I stuck with this cooking. And the relationship with my kid's mother was at a point where we didn't really dig each other. We thought we wanted it to work but it wasn't working. I didn't want to go back to the streets or whatever.

So, I knew at one time another lady that I had an eye for. I kinda like met her and got in touch with her. We was just hooking up, like going out, having a drink and just talking because she was vulnerable and I was vulnerable. But we didn't really getting hooked up or nothing. We were just hanging out. And we were just liking each other. So, I would meet her somewhere. And I didn't have a car. And me and my kid's mother was cool. I used to drive her car. But I'm working, trying to get on my feet. So, I really was not willing to date. I really would try to make things work with my kid's mother but it wasn't working. So, I was just looking for an opportunity to find a good woman that really got something going on. That I could bring to the table and we could build something and we could share the future together. That's the type of relationship I was looking for because I was messed up because I had all the things that I did, always mess up.

CHAPTER 44

Now, me and my new lady friend started hanging out. We would hook up every other weekend. I would spend time with my daughter. Me and my kid's mother still live together. And we were just really co-parenting. We was trying to be in a relationship that she sure have funny ways of showing it. So, I was being patient with her. We didn't have sex or nothing like that. I slept in the guest room. And that was that. We would go to work. She would go her way and I would go my way but we got along. But patience with me was running out because I was trying to see what level we was on. And she was more of a homebody and I was still like an outgoing because I wasn't trying to really be at home. I was trying to really get on my feet because my incarceration, I sat down for 18 months and I had a plan to upgrade myself. I'm working but time was moving fast. So, I was just trying to motivate myself to do better. And I really thought that the lady, my kid's mother, the lady I live with, is co-parenting, that we was going to build a future together but it didn't work out that way.

So, I started seeing my new lady friend and we was hanging out. Other weekends, we would go for a couple hours, go to a bar to eat and talk and laugh a little bit. And I would let her know my situation. And she respected it because I kept it real with her. I told her I lived with my kid's mother. And she had her own house. She had broke up with her guy and she lived by herself. And I can go over her house. She invited me over her house. She had her own house. So, I go by there and we would just kick it over there and drink and I would meet her kids. She had three daughters and a son and I had three daughters and a son. It was a coincidence that turned out like that. So, it kind of made me have a very good interest in finding her attractive that we could be real some because I let her know things about me, she let me know things about her. We all had a past of negative energy but we try to move on. We didn't bring that to the table. I would not talk about my past because I was incarcerated and I was a bad boy and I was a street guy and she was a homebody just like my kid's mother but she would go to work every day just like my kid's mother. But she was a little bit more spontaneous. We will have fun and hang out and laugh. We had a lot in common.

We knew some of the same people also but that's what made me and her really started liking each other. And then also that her kids, I met her kids and her kids started accepting me too. Because once you win the kids over, everything works out. So, her daughters, they had a good judgmental opinion about they was very protective about their mother, who she date because she went through a breakup with her ex-husband. And so, they was just real skeptical and she was too. I got a stamp approval from her kids saying that I was a good guy so that let me in the door. We weren't serious yet but they saying he's a cool guy. In other words, so we would continue seeing each other. But I was more devoted to my youngest daughter because I didn't want to lose that bond with her because we did so much stuff together and she was getting older. So, I was just trying to be a better father at the same time but I had to do things for myself to make me happy.

CHAPTER 45

As I take this journey to get ready for work and wake my daughter up and get her ready for school., she's sleeping next to me. Her mother come in from work and get her ready. As I get myself ready and leave out and walk to Warrensville Center to take the 48, right here on South Miles in Warrensville Center and take me to Van Aken Train Station to catch the train to downtown to cross over and get on the next train, take it to the west side and take me to West 117th. Sometimes the bus will come right straight across 117th. And it usually dropped me right off where I work at on Lake Ave at the Pier W. I began walking because I don't like to wait. So, I like to keep my thinking process going as I make this journey of getting back on my feet. I go to a restaurant; it's called Pier W. It sits on top of a nice rock, offshore from the Lake Erie that you can see downtown Cleveland. It's real cozy and elegant where it's upscale, where people come to eat a nice seafood dinner. We got a lot of celebrities coming there, football players, basketball players, baseball players and some actors at times when they come to Cleveland. I was very proud of myself to have this job. I began by lying on my application because I really wanted this job. And I know that I can cook and they don't sell feathers and I just come home from the penitentiary. And I did what I had to do.

CHAPTER 46

2012, I'm enjoying myself at the new job as a cook. But as the days go by and months go by, I started to observe the people that I worked with because I was the only black person that worked in the kitchen at this time. I mean, they would look at me in a certain kind of way. But I pay that no attention because this business is not personal. They make it personal because they feel like they are better than me. Like, I don't know nothing but I prove myself. But still I can't win because I'm outnumbered in the kitchen. So, I get in where I fit in and being myself. And I am just glad that I got through some of the things that I've been through to change my life. It was hard but I made the best of a bad situation. And what I mean by that, my social life was still unbalanced. I had to get that right. Because I really wasn't in a place to really be serious with my new lady friend.

Because, I didn't have nothing to bring to the table at that time. So, I'm just doing my one-two. Well, she understood but she get to really liking my character and the potentials that I got. And me and my kid's mother, my youngest daughter, we would do things. And as far as being a family-orientated co-parenting, we have fun and we laugh and joke. But at the end of the day, the love and attention in the house wasn't there. And that make me more aware that I had to get on my feet and get my own place. Now, my new lady friend want me to move in with her. I was hesitant because she was really into me now. And I'm really into her. So, I just take one day at a time and I just spend a night over her house, on every other weekend. And I at least had a couple outfits over there. So basically, she know that she is moving me in slowly for sure.

CHAPTER 47

So now, the next day, my kid's mother went down to Virginia to Commonwealth City to find out what's going on with my son. She gave me a call to let me know and his recovery of being shot that I talked to him. I was relieved. And I told him to take it easy until I come home and we'll talk about it. So, my prayers was answered. God wasn't ready for him to take my son home. And the family, the sisters was relieved also. So, now I can go on with my journey because my prayer's been answered. And I wait till my son returned back to Ohio. And we can talk about what happened and to change your way of thinking to be a better person. I know the apple don't fall from the tree because my son was a hustler just like his father but he didn't do drugs like I did. He learned a different way, a different pattern. Because what he knew that his father was going through, he tried to do it in a different way. But tried to be successful because the struggles that I went through, it is hurting my son and my kids.

And I tell them when they get older more to understand what I went through and how I got exposed to negative energy and being a follower of being cool and I end up making bad decisions and getting hooked on drugs. But the outcome was, God had another plan for me. I just had to stay strong and survive it. I learned the hard way by going through penitentiary four times. I have four numbers. And that's not something to brag about. And I know that one day, I would find a road to success if I put my mind to it, to be a better person. I'm really into this culinary cooking thing. It really kept me grounded and not. I love what I do with my hands to be creative. Like I say, the food was like an art and the food that you make, you can just want people to compliment you. It makes me feel good. I like the compliments when I make the food just right.

So, now my journey is to take it to another level. But I have to find the right people to help me start my business because I don't wanna work in a corporate world. I want to work for myself. That had always been my dream to be independent but it's hard. It ain't what you know, it's who you know. So, my craft, I try to promote myself but I got a lot of turn downs because people didn't believe in me or supported me and it really hurt me because I tried to create my craft and go to the other level and I was just feeling like maybe I'm making bad decisions or not networking enough to take it to another level. I really didn't know how to network. But it's the same thing as selling drugs in the streets. And I had to use that kind of thing, a hustling tactic to really get myself off the ground. It was a slow process. So, I just had to leave it like that for now.

CHAPTER 48

My son made it back to Ohio. His mother brought him home. I was relieved but me going to work every day, grinding and me and my new girlfriend. And staying prayed up and just focused on the positive things in life, like, me going to work, keeping my head above water and staying out of trouble. So, my son, I was going to get around and talk to him when he got home but I waited till he get healed all the way because I know he got his mother and his two sisters and his grandmother and people around him was going to care until him nursing back to health. So, it's been about a month for I have seen him. So, it's like about the beginning of November, I go by and check on him and this was time for me and him to talk and he tell me his part of what happened. I was crushed about he living a dangerous life, hustling. And I was hurt that somebody set him up and it was somebody that was close. And I told him in this game of the street hustling, you ain't got no friends. You can't trust no one. Because that greed for money, once you see a person doing gooder than you, they don't want to see you do better than them. And they'll do whatever it takes.

I know he understand that because he is an intelligent young man but that's part of the territory of being in the streets. So now, I fall back and let my son be the man he's supposed to be. And I end up working another job. Just going on 2014 now. An offer came up. One of the guys I knew had a bar and he wanted me to run the kitchen. And this was in Cleveland Heights. I had to go check it out and see what kind of clientele it is. It was a small kitchen. But the people in there was like neighborhood people. It wasn't an upscale bar; it was just a neighborhood bar. But I'm checking out the atmosphere and I meet the people that's in there. And a friend of mine said, well, can you change it around? Because he just bought this place. And I'm like, well, yes, I can. And so, I'm putting back what I seen in the bar. And I just thought about, now this is my time to shine. And the guy didn't want to, he said, you ain't gotta pay me nothing. Just get on your feet and Imma let you eat. I just want you to serve good food and bring good clientele in and you make a name for yourself.

So, I was like, all right, cool. You just buy your own food and take care of your business. So, I thought about it and I said, wow! It's time for me to leave the yacht club because my opportunity started to change. For me, this is like always something I really wanted to do and just starting in a bar is a stepping stone for me to see what I'm really made of. So now, my creativity came in. I go to work. I left the yacht club and took on this bar to be independent of myself. And when I put my menu together, people start to come in and check my food out. Once they start testing my food, the word spread and I'm good at what I do when it come to that food. So now, I seeing the people's face and they're like, wow, we've been waiting for somebody like you to really come in this part of the neighborhood. And the bar location was on Noble Road in Cleveland Heights.

And the word got around fast because the guy that I knew and one of my guys that I grew up with, they telling the people. They were like, oh! D got some good food; you should support him. And now I'm shocked. I'm, like, in the small kitchen, I'm doing $300-$400 a day, six days a week. That's good money, tax free. I'm real proud of myself. My profit was like a couple hundred dollars but me buying my food, I buy fresh food because it was a small bar and it had a small kitchen. But it was cool. I'm doing my thing. And now I'm seeing all kinds of people come there from all over to buy my food. And I'm feeling on top of the world to just sell bar food. And I'm really impressed. And like I say, my

105

numbers was doing good. I felt good about myself and I was like, wow. This is how it is to be an entrepreneur. And it was draining but it was worth it. I'm meeting all kinds of people that I knew from the streets. I'm just saying that, good people to get with, good energy.

CHAPTER 49

So, the bar is doing real good. I'm really going to a next level. My profit increase, I'm making, like, $300 overhead a day and people loving my food. I start work at, I open up at 12, all the way to 01 o'clock at night. I'm grinding. I'm really doing what I gotta do. The people will call me and my dude that run the bar. He would call me so much and ask me where I'm at. And I'll be doing the food shopping. Because I get up early in the morning about 9 or 10 and do the food shopping and I tell him I will be there. He would be like they only want no drinks. They really want the food at lunch time. I had a line. I was so impressed. I had a line out the door wanting my food. And I was like wow. And I had all kinds of workers that come there that really supported me. I was very, very impressed. I'm telling my new girlfriend how I felt about it. And she was happy for me. And everything going good. I had a good run for it, a year. Now, the guy that owned the bar, he got into some financial problems with the bar. So, he didn't really let me know. So, I'm done. A guy come in and bought the bar. And he didn't even tell me to the last minute.

And he told the guy about me, my guy that run the kitchen, he is cool. Let him keep the kitchen. But the guy that run the bar said he got his own staff. I don't need him. So, this would took the topping off the cake. When that hit, I was so upset because he left me in the dark. And I was really hurt. So, I had to go back to a nine to five. And I was hurt. It took me a while but I had to just sit back and weigh my options. And

I left it like that for 2014. Went on 2015. It was all good because like I just say, I was trying to save enough money to really get that bar because I was doing real good. I like, about a year or two, I probably would have kind of brought that bar because I knew what he wanted for the bar but another hustler come in and buy it. And money talk, bull shit walk. So, he knew what it was, he knew what the clientele was when I was in there but he didn't want to see me eat. So, I had to cash out and get up out of there.

CHAPTER 50

I'd like to dedicate this book to my kids, my four kids. My son Daryl, my daughter Tateesha, my daughter Tanisha, my daughter, Taylor. I just want you to get some understanding of what your dad went through and where I'm going and what I've accomplished to this day. I changed my life for the best because I love my kids and I realize that life is short and I'm trying to be the best version of me. I changed for the best and I'm feeling good about myself and without God, I can't do this without him. I learned the hard way but now that I adjust and got my life back together, I'm winning now. Much love, Dad.

www.ingramcontent.com/pod-product-compliance
Lightning Source LLC
Chambersburg PA
CBHW021121130626
46554CB00002B/803